AFRICAN AMERICAN FAMILY LIFE:.
(It's Time To Get It Back)

Rosalind M. Stanley

xulon
PRESS

...he who sows righteousness reaps a sure reward.
Proverbs 11:18b

The fruit of righteousness will be peace...
Isaiah 32:17

This book is dedicated to my Father, Jehovah God. The One in whom I live and move and have my being. The Creator and Sustainer of all things. The One who originated Family Life from the beginning and who sent His Son, The Lord Jesus Christ AKA The Word, that families would have the freedom to turn to Him and engage in His way of doing things.

And

To African American families everywhere, "we had it, we lost it, and we gotta' get it back," that is, our sincere dependence upon God, our commitment to living for Him and accountability to our local churches. This is what made us in America, this is what sustained us, this is what we so desperately need to help our children and children's children grasp in their hearts, what is just, right and pleasing to God to know His peace and Presence.

Table of Contents

Acknowledgments

"In all your ways acknowledge Him and He will direct your path." Proverbs 3:6

Lord, I acknowledge you as the author and finisher of my faith and of everything that concerns me. I acknowledge your goodness and kindness in my life that has led me to salvation and friendship with You. Thank you for all that you have done, ensuring that I have a family to share love and life with, including the family of God. I acknowledge that *because of your grace* extended to me, this book has come to be. Thank you, Lord.

To the wonderful people who helped me during graduate school, with my first seminar geared to the African American family at Regent University in Virginia Beach, Virginia. I appreciate you: Muriel Agard, Charlotte Alford, Patricia Burpo, Betty Dixon, Mary Case, Laverne Grant, Dexter Harris, Daryl Leonard, Russell West, Drew Van Houten, Scott & Marylyn Dixon, other members of Regent Student Outreach and New Generation Fellowship, Bishop Wellington Boone and ministers from his ministry. To Regent University staff who assisted our efforts including Mitch Baker, David Martin and Heinz Schoenhoff. For supervising my work as this seminar became my thesis project, Bishop B. Courtney McBath and Dr. George Jefferson, thank you. You will always hold a special place in my heart. Thanks, also, to Cindy Brewer and Decie

Rowlands for your excellent typing and proofing skills.

I must acknowledge the friend that I gained as a result of this work, Clarence Shuler. Clarence, I thank you for your encouragement and those words of confirmation, "It is time to get out of the boat." *For such a time as this...* I'm out and hopefully will not need a towel.

Thanks also to Dr. James Dobson and the staff at Focus on the Family who appreciated my original work. I am finally doing it! Your comments encouraged me.

I acknowledge Elders David Yeazell and William Purcell for their diligence and excellence in developing The Potter's Institute of Dallas, Texas and their encouragement in allowing me to teach some of this material. Also, much thanks to my brother, Elder Bobby Gibson for your vote of confidence in allowing Art & I to teach some aspects of this material as we facilitated the Potter's House Counseling Department's Marriage Enrichment Group. We were more blessed to see the changes taking place in many of the marriages. To Bishop TD Jakes, First Lady Serita Jakes and the Pastors and Leaders of The Potter's House Church of Dallas, Texas, I acknowledge you and your determination to teach biblical principles to families around the world. Thank you for all that you have imparted to Arthur and I.

What would I have done without my family members: The Williams', Caldwell's, Generals', Moreno's, Dominguez's and Stanley's, and all those connected to these family names (aunts, uncles, cousins, in-laws), I acknowledge and thank you for just being you. We have had our good times and our not so good times, but "we are family." Thank you for the lessons that I have learned and the growth that has come in all of our lives through our implementation of God's ways into our relationships.

I owe more than I can pay in dollars to my wonderful prayer warring mother, Rosetta Caldwell and my precious daughter, Victoria Dominquez, for taking the time to edit and proofread. Mostly, thank you for being such friends and a support to me. That goes to my sisters, Cookie (Linda Lee) and Dawn, my brothers, Kenny and Lenny, my son, Jason, who just a few days ago gave me a Proverbs 31: 28 compliment to my face. Cookie, without your kindness and grace, I would not have been able to seize the divine moment for publishing this book.

To my favorite aunts and my uncle: Shirley, Lola, Edna, Uncle Bob, and a host of other relatives and friends (Dr. Paris Finner-Williams, Dr. Priscilla Drew-Souza, Carolyn Ross, Bobby Gibson and staff, Brenda Davis, Tim Thompson, Dwight and Joyce Linyear, Betty Dixon, Pat Burpo, Terry Whitfield-Lassiter, Ray & Audrey Holloway, Pastor & Mrs. Kykendall & Agape Christian Church of Paterson, NJ, Andrea Adams, Dr. Diaris Bates-Jackson, Marylyn Dixon, Pastor & Mrs. Stevenson & Greenway Church of Fort Worth, Texas, Teresa McCrimmon, Carolyn Milbourne, Debe Loving, Sharon Manuel, Sherry Douglas, Nancy Alcorn, Juretha Phillips, Queen Mims, Helen Wilson, Fredda Jenkins, Daryl and Rose Woodruff, Ron and Debbie Copleland, Nat and Anna Tate, Rose Hunt, Anne Hunt, Debra Winans, Denise Gray, Joyce Spratlen, to name only a few of the awesome friends that God has blessed me with) who God planted in my path at designated times in my life to remind me that I had something from God to give to others. You guys have kept me going many of those times that I wanted to throw in the towel.

As for the anointed pastors that God blessed me with along my road of spiritual growth, (still on the road) Albert P. Rowe, Clinton & Sarah Utterbach, William Saunders, B. Courtney & Janeen McBath, and T.D Jakes. Thank you does not nearly express my gratitude for the great spiritual impartation you have made in my life and the life changing instruction that helped me move from ungodly to godly living! I have to give honor, thanks and appreciation to my spiritual dad, Dr. Zin White, Jr. and his spiritually gifted wife, Irma. From the time that we met, those many years ago, you filled a father void that I did not realize I had. Thanks for being available whenever we call on you! Special thanks to Pastor Tom Iannucci of Breath of Life Christian Ministries, (on the island of Kauai in Hawaii) for your awesome teaching and for helping me at a critical moment by letting me use your computer to finalize this book. We are blessed to know You, D'Lissa, and the Breath of Life family!

Saving the best for last, Arthur, God gave me you at the right time, He knows best. Thank you for choosing to make me your best friend and choosing to live God's way. Our marriage and family relationships, though not perfect, are proof positive that when we do it God's way, His joy, peace and Presence remains with us, leads us, and sustains us especially through the hard times. I love you more than my words can express and am ever so proud to be your wife!

Preface

"My people are destroyed for lack of knowledge"

The purpose of this writing is to serve as a means and a guide to assist African Americans in gaining a better understanding of themselves and their heritage and to recognize the reasons for misunderstandings, misrepresentations, generational curses and the continual demise of the African American family. Furthermore, to enable African American families to begin to prosper in all areas of living and family life through an introduction to the biblical model for life and living.

African Americans are one of the few people groups who have had a number of name changes within a few decades; Colored, Negro, Black, Afro-American, to now African American. This is evidence of a people not fully certain of who they are. This identity discrepancy can lead a people to a sense of insecurity, instability, and hopelessness.

Many historians have said that if a person does not know where they are from, they will not know how to determine where they are going. They are apt to make the same mistakes continually because they have not had the opportunity to learn from their past errors. Further, if a person does not know who they are, they will remain in a search process looking for themselves in other people or through what they do.

Knowledge of the past is not only powerful, it is critical to the growth of any people. It is vitally important to the growth of a people in a wholistic sense. Without proper knowledge of their past, destruction of a people's culture and values will ensue. This writing therefore, will attempt to provide a summation of the history of the African American family along with a brief history of the African American church and its' influence. It will then provide a biblical mandate on family life and living, generally and specifically.

We are currently living in an age in which the younger generation, in many cases, do not know their own family history let alone the history of their people. According to the latest statistics, many African American youth (about 40%) have not experienced living in a home with their own father and mother. African Americans represent 12% of the population of America. Almost 50% of that population are one-parent family homes run mainly by females as head of household.

Some of the children of these homes do not have a personal relationship with their biological fathers. Those who do, in many cases, have inadequate involvement with them and/or an undeveloped parent/child relationship. This in itself should cause alarm as we see the number of African American youth turning to gangs and other inappropriate behaviors to meet their need for direction, guidance, love, attention, and affection.

A newer phenomenon is that of African American mothers turning to drug use as a way of escaping the pain or burden often experienced when child-rearing alone. Some mothers simply decide that they do not want the stress so leave their children to be reared by a family member or friend. The catch 22 situation of not having the skills to get a better job, not having the financial or emotional support to get further training, or leaving children home alone as they work extra hours, overwhelms some parents causing them to eventually become helpless, hopeless or to quit trying. The children begin to become neglected in some way and end up with growth deficits that hinder their progress in life.

Many children are given to their mother's mother to nurture and to rear. This poses a problem in that many of the grandmothers are not in a position either financially, emotionally or physically to take on the full responsibility for their grandchildren. This often puts the children in a vulnerable position in which they begin to make decisions for their lives sooner then they are mentally or emotionally capable.

Although teen pregnancy rates have declined, young Black females are still two to three times more likely then White females to conceive during their adolescent years," states Black Women's Health Imperative (Fact Sheet, 2001). Immature females are rearing children without the appropriate knowledge or understanding of the role and responsibility of a mother. Educational goals become less important as child rearing becomes more of a focus for these young women. The Black male/female "issue" has been a long discussed problem causing misunderstandings and inappropriate role modeling for the younger generation. Not to mention the same sex relationships and the impact they will have on future generations.

The criminal justice system is inundated with African American males. Many of these males are products of fatherless homes. Many of these males are fathers themselves and do not have the tools, ability, or availability to serve as proper role models to their own children. Many of them have become involved in the drug scene as a means of survival in their environment. Many are serving prison terms unjustifiably longer than the actual crime warranted. Many of the children of these men become a part of a continual cycle of defeat.

These and other factors are proof that the African American family is in a state of crisis. Such as is the case in any crisis, if the proper decisions are not made and implemented in a specified amount of time, the crisis will begin to maintain itself in inappropriate and destructive ways. It is time for the Christ-centered church to intervene. The crisis situation in the African American community requires Divine intervention through solid biblical instruction to bring about positive changes. Lasting change can only come about through the application of these biblical principles in family life.

This book is written with a goal to incite people to action, especially those committed to being the Love and Light that God has chosen His people to be. It is the responsibility of Christians to "go" to the aid of African American families in crisis, especially African American Christians, to preach the Gospel—God's way of living, to bring righteousness, peace and joy to a chaotic situation.

Introduction

*"There is a way that seems right to man,
but the end leads to destruction."
Proverbs 14:12 & 16: 25*

Family life in today's society has many meanings depending upon who is giving the definition. Therefore, we see many kinds of behavior taking place in families. A clear understanding of God's way for family life is lacking in many American families. Consequently, many families go about their daily living in an ignorance that leads to destruction.

Children are growing up with a false understanding of living and improper expectations for life. Christian parents are yielding to what secular society says is right or wrong without question or challenge. Marriages are crumbling like never before and out of wedlock pregnancies are at an all-time high in the African American community, (Index of Leading Cultural Indicators, p.44), and of significant mention America's drastic turn toward same sex marriages and the millions of abortions taking place yearly.

How do we stop the madness that has permeated our society? How do we help heal the sadness of many people today due to unfulfilled expectations in relationships? What do we say to children who are stuck in negative situations out of their control? What will happen to the many marriages starting and ending without the proper foundation? How do we encourage the younger generation to believe that marriage can work and can last? These are some of the questions that the second half of this book is intended to address.

From a personal perspective, I have experienced a negative family life as well as a positive family life. Positive is better. It is harder work, but it works. It requires a decision to apply the principles of God. To last, a decision to live for God is required. That is, giving your life and the lives and lifestyle of your family to Him, yielding to His way of doing things.

Regardless as to the variation of family that your family unit represents (one parent, two parent, grandparent and grandchildren, aunt, uncle and niece, or blended family), God's way appropriately applied will make the difference between healthy versus unhealthy, functional versus dysfunctional, connected versus disconnected and godly versus ungodly family relationships. The application of biblical principles will positively affect generations of family members after you.

My prayer is that this not just be a book that you have read. Instead, that it serves as a manual to help you to better understand how to effectively apply God's way for living. That it is an assistant to you as you choose to implement His way into your *family life* or as you use it to assist others. My sincerest desire is that you receive revelation from the Spirit of God that will inspire and empower you in *putting God's way into action and getting back what we lost!*

Because of God's amazing Grace...

Roz Stanley

CHAPTER ONE

An Overview

"Looking at the past (if assessed wisely)
helps to secure a positive future that will last."

The African American family is in a state of disarray. The current state of African Americans and their family situation in particular, cannot be fully understood without a historical perspective (Newton, 1988, p.4). "Any serious effort to understand the many changes in African American family life...must be pursued within the framework which recognizes that the whole of African American family life is greater than any of its parts. This proposition is 'holistic' in the sense that it encompasses African American structure and functioning in all its variety" (Billingsley, 1990, p.85). As we trace the history of the African American family, we find that there has been some form of disjointing since the arrival of Africans in America for the purpose of slavery.

Since Africans were disallowed the freedom to maintain family relationships and cultural ties upon their arrival to America, African Americans as a nation of people, from the onset, began to lose family and cultural tradition. This has caused a state of disorientation amongst the African American community and families of America. "The black man was brought to this country forcibly and was completely cut off from his past. He was robbed of language and culture. He was forbidden to be African and not allowed to be American" (Banks, 1972, p.13).

A closer look at this history reveals that the African American church, as far back as slavery, has been of great influence in providing instruction and direction to the African American family. African Americans that were not converted to the Christian faith looked with respect to the church and the church ministers for advice and instruction.

In most cases, the African American church served as a means for family survival. "An organized religious life became the chief means by which a structured or organized social life came into existence among the masses. This provided an organization in Negro life which has persisted until the present time" (Frazier, 1963, p.31)

As the free African American population increased and the eventual emancipation of slaves occurred, many began to migrate to the cities of America. This required an adjustment to a new and different environment and lifestyle. The rural church was not in a position to minister to the needs of the people in the city.

Even though African American churches began to be established in the cities, the influence of the church upon family life began to decrease and family disorder began to increase. "The most important crisis of the Negro migrant was produced by the absence of the church which had been the center of his social life and refuge from a hostile world" (Frazier, 1963, p.48).

E. Franklin Frazier, a noted historian, goes on to say that this migration to the cities, especially in the north, resulted in a shift from the church as a balancing unit. This brought about a change in the religious behaviors of African Americans that has continued well into the twenty first century.

Due to lack of order, biblically speaking, in much of the African American community, much role confusion exists. There is a dire need for biblical instruction regarding family life. Even though there may have been a lack of rooting and grounding of family tradition and accurate knowledge of African American history for many African American families, the truth and order found in The Bible, God's Word to man, is able to save from destruction and demise.

Biblical instruction about family living along with the teaching of African American history can bring about a stability that will not fail. "God made well-being and happiness of the family dependent upon the observation of His divinely appointed order. Any change from that order only brings forth a misshapen form, for which there is no cure except a return to God's order" (Christenson, 1970, p.18)

Therefore, this writer contends that a useful means to bring order to African American families and communities is with biblical instruction through the presentation of seminars that are specifically geared to their needs. Such workshops or seminars should be in conjunction with or sponsored by Christ-centered churches in America.

An important function of these seminars would be to assist African American churches in providing accurate and adequate biblical instruction regarding family relationships. The goal is that of strengthening families spiritually which will empower them toward progress and prosperity in all areas of life.

The information in this book is presented to provide guidance, structure, and tools for those with a willingness of heart and desire to be used as an agent of change. Hopefully, after reading you will choose to join in the fight in bringing lasting change to families and communities in your realm of influence. The goal is to impact individuals, families and communities with godly wisdom and knowledge that can aid them in making the necessary changes for a productive and prosperous family life.

CHAPTER TWO

The African American Family

"God is not through with us yet..."

Even though Africans participated in European exploits in the New World from the beginning, (Franklin, 1980, p.30), the first African Americans to settle in America were brought over as indentured servants (Banks, 1972, p.12). As indentured servants, they served the European settlers for approximately seven years then became free men.

Very little is known about the lives and later happenings of these twenty Africans because records concerning them were not kept. As the demand for African labor increased, the restrictions placed upon possible freedom after serving also increased. Eventually, the idea of African slavery became a reality because Africans, as opposed to Native Americans, were easier to keep track of due to skin color and the fact that they were foreigners in the land.

Although the importation of African slaves began as far back as 1517, the slave trade did not become an official practice in America until the 1700's. Africans at times sold other Africans into American slavery who had served as slaves for their particular tribe and American slave traders stole Africans from their land.

Whatever family and communal life that existed among Africans prior to their being brought to America began to be destroyed before they even landed in America, by way of the separation that the slave trade demanded. They were separated from friends and family soon after their arrival in America, usually by two's, thus, making the meeting up of kinsmen unlikely (Frazier, 1966, pp.5-7).

Customs, languages, and memories of the African culture were not allowed to take root in the New World. Most slave owners would not allow any semblance of the African heritage for fear of uprising. Thus, the African slave had to learn a new language and culture while memories of the old culture quickly vanished. "In most Black American families where there is knowledge of African origins, it became a more or less vague part of family traditions" (Frazier, 1966, p.10)

E. Franklin Frazier, a reputable historian of African American history, stated "probably never before in history has a people been so nearly completely stripped of its' social heritage as the Negroes who were brought to America" (Frazier, 1966, p.15)

The existence of a family life amongst the slave population depended largely upon their labor status. Due to economics, male slaves were usually set up as stallions while many female slaves served as channels for the reproduction of more slaves. This practice was not congenial to the development of love and commitment between the male and female slave. Once children were born, they often were sold to other slave owners.

The difference between being a field hand and a house servant often played a major role in determining whether or not a family remained together, were separated or even allowed to act as a family. The temperament of the slave owner and his outlook upon his slaves was a major factor in slave family life taking root.

Although the love, commitment, and protection that comes with family life was discouraged among slaves, the bond between mother and child often remained strong. This bond, at times, was so strong that a mother would die attempting to keep her child. There were also many instances wherein the slave father separated from his family would persist unto death to return to them.

Slavery had a devastating effect upon African American male and female relationships. The slave owner very often degraded the male and elevated the female. This was a tactic used to emasculate the African American male. The seed that was planted in the conscience and heart of the African American male remains a battleground to this day (Newton, 1988, p. 29).

The mother or female became the most valuable and indispensable member of the family (Newton, 1988, p.12). Even after emancipation, many women maintained the role as the depended upon person in the family as they were employed at a higher rate than the African American male.

Emancipation did, however, bring about somewhat of a role change for the African American male. Due to the new economic system, the male found himself in position as authority figure in his family (Frazier, 1966, p. 129). Many Whites placed responsibility upon the male, for example, to pay the rent.

Soon after World War I, African Americans began to move in droves to the cities due to the great need for unskilled labor in factories. The shift from the rural environment to the cluttered city environment, especially in the north, imposed major adjustments upon the family, which often led to a breakdown in family relationships.

This new lifestyle in the urban setting was cold and impersonal, unlike that to which most of these African Americans were accustomed. They began to develop attitudes, values, and practices consistent with this new way of life without the once essential influence of the family church and the family atmosphere that was created in the rural setting. These entities served as a means of social control in the rural environment.

In this new setting, women were in a better position than men in finding and maintaining employment. This, in some cases, was a cause for men to leave their families because of a sense of helplessness and loss of dignity. Children as a result, were left to themselves more as mothers spent many hours out of the home working. This led to much juvenile delinquency.

This new freedom was a great challenge for the African American family, especially for those that were not accustomed to a consistent pattern of family life. Sexual promiscuity, during this time, became the norm for many African Americans, male and female. Men and women would live together outside of marriage, then move on to different partners, as they desired. Since marital commitment and husband/wife relationships were not the norm during slavery, these newly freed African Americans had no real basis or understanding in this area.

There were, however, free African Americans during slavery who did establish and maintain consistent family lives. Ex-slaves who were able to set up acceptable marriage and family relationships were able to do so because of exposure to their slave master's family life or a vague remembrance of tribal life. Many slaves, however, were not given the opportunity to observe their master's family life.

Much of the behavior of African Americans after slavery was like that of a child let loose by parents to live as adults without the necessary home training. "The removal of the authority of masters after Emancipation caused promiscuous sex relations to become widespread and permitted constant changing of spouses. This was due to separation of husband and wife during slavery and the social disorganization that resulted from Emancipation" (Frazier, 1963, p.32).

At this time, many missionaries from the north and Europe came to evangelize the newly freed African American to teach them about marriage from a legal standpoint. Legal marriage had not been a part of the slave value system (Frazier, 1963, p.32).

Child rearing in the urban setting required a new set of standards, which was quite different from the standard of the Caucasian middle class norms. Economics caused parents to devise patterns of socialization predicated upon the principle that children in the urban setting must be taught to survive in a hostile society (Newton, 1988, p.21).

The African American family has faced many challenges since arriving in America. Family disorientation continues to this day. This is not to discount the many stable and successful African American families from slavery up to the current century. The focus of this writing is upon the African American family at large and the African American families living in crisis situations as the norm.

The next section will examine the importance of the church throughout the history of African Americans. Much of the morality and cohesiveness of many African American families today would not have been possible without the influence of the church (Newton, 1988, p.9).

CHAPTER THREE

The African American Church

"Now we know that we, the people, are the church"

The African American church is and has been a supportive institution to the African American family and the African American community for many years. However, as noted by Newton in 1988, "the black traditional church is spiritually weak and suffers from biblical ignorance and moral depravity –this extends to the white traditional church as well" (p.2). Though now in the twenty first century many of our African American churches teach more biblically than in the past, a history of the African American church is appropriate.

The beginnings of the African American church goes as far back as slavery when some slave owners introduced their slaves to the Christian religion. This new religion provided the basis for cohesion for the newly arrived African. In the eighteenth century a systematic attempt was made on the part of the Church of England to Christianize Africans in America (Frazier, 1963, p.6).

What later became known as the African American church has its roots among enslaved African Americans. It was termed "the invisible institution" (Frazier, 1963, p.13). The preacher was usually a plantation worker who had gained some knowledge of the Bible and had an experience with God, which "called" him into the office. The requirements to preach were: knowledge of scripture, ability to speak and communicate his knowledge to the other slaves, as well as the ability to sing (Frazier, 1963, pp.17-18). Preaching consisted of dramatizing the stories of the Bible.

Although slaves were not allowed to congregate for worship without a reputable white man present, they somehow found ways to assemble together to praise and worship God without the invasion of the overseer. Often times, slaves would attend church with their masters, basically so that the slave owner could keep watch over them. However, some slave owners would dramatize the Bible for their slaves.

"The Christian religion drew slaves into union with their fellowman and tended to break down the barriers that isolated them morally from their white masters. Participation in the same religious service drew the slave out of moral isolation in a white man's world" (Frazier, 1963, p.9).

The invisible institution and the free African American church that existed during slavery and after the Civil War, joined together after slavery out of a need for ministry amongst the newly freed slaves. This joining together brought a level of structure and organization into the lives of African American families that persists to the present. This "organized religious life became the chief means by which a structured or organized social life came into existence among the Negro masses" (Frazier, 1963, pp.30-31). The church became and remained until the 1940's, the agency for social control among African Americans.

"The church was the source from which Blacks gained a sense of identity" (Newton, 1988, p.9). It allowed men the opportunity to experience leadership and authority, roles that they were not allowed in society. "It promoted psychological liberation, leadership development, intellectuality, equipping of families for their roles at home, equipping men with good stewardship methods and social networking" (Newton, 1988, pp.13-14).

Mutual aid societies developed out of the church. African Americans would pool their meager resources to buy land and buildings to house the institution that became the center of family and social life. Preachers greatly influenced the social, political, and educational lives of the African American communities, as they were usually the community leaders.

The first African American churches were founded in 1773 in South Carolina and 1776 in Virginia. The Free African Society was established in 1786 by Richard Allen and Absalom Jones. Both had been members of a white congregation. During one church service they mistakenly kneeled to pray in the wrong section and were dragged out of the church. As a result they left and started an African American church. Due to a disagreement in style of worship Jones then organized the African Protestant Episcopal Church of St. Thomas (Frazier, 1963, p.27).

In 1816, by Allen's initiation, A.M.E. (African Methodist Episcopalian) churches were established in other cities. Later, a group of blacks in New York organized the Zion church out of which came the A.M.E. Zion church. Also, independent Baptist churches were being established as well as other denominational churches (Frazier, 1963, p.28).

One of the oldest Baptist churches in the United States was the result of the efforts of George Liele, a former slave, which became The African Baptist Church of Georgia (Frazier, 1963, p.23).

When African Americans increasingly began to move to northern cities during World War I, a severe breakdown in the family ensued. The traditional southern, rural oriented church was not able to minister to the needs of the urban African American family. "Secularization of black churches took place and they began to focus their attention upon the black man's condition in the world" (Frazier, 1963, p.50).

Their interest in worldly affairs caused the African American church to begin to preach what is called a "social gospel" rather than the Gospel of Jesus Christ (Banks, 1972, p.91). As a result, notes Newton, "the black family has been left spiritually weakened and unable to deal with the worldly forces of humanism" (Newton, 1988, p.2).

From the early 50's to the Twenty First Century, the African American church has grown and has experienced much change. The 60's brought the Civil Rights Movement where preachers, such as Dr Martin Luther King, Jr., held center stage and served as a positive role model to many African American churches and community as a whole. The 60's and 70's introduced many African American's to the Nation of Islam, the American Muslim religion that taunted Christianity as the white man's religion.

Many African Americans were also introduced to the Jehovah's Witness religion, which argues against the reality of the Trinity, which is a major belief of Christianity. Both religions provided the structure that had been weakened in many African American churches, however, they have not been able to provide the inner solace and community unity experienced by African American church goers of the past.

As the 60's through to the 90's brought about a more individual-istic mentality in American as a whole, Christianity as the African American religion was questioned and many African Americans individually decided to experiment with other religions. Spirituality became a coined phrase for a religious experiment rather than rela-tionship with God through Jesus Christ.

In the Twenty First century, there appears to be a return to Christianity and to the church. The danger or progress in the return rests in motives. Many are convinced that financial prosperity and freedom from an impoverished life will come through outward behaviors, which man controls, not recognizing or understanding the primary goal of a Christian life. Entering into the kind of rela-tionship with God that changes a person and a family's internal and external world is the most important ingredient to this noted return. This is the proposition and goal of this writing, that African American families would return to our "First Love." (Revelations 2:4) Let's consider what it will take for African American marriages and families to *get back what has been lost.*

CHAPTER FOUR

Time for Action,
Time for Change

"Let us not just be hearers only...but doers of what we hear"

From our brief review of the African American family and the African American church, it is obvious that strong measures need to be implemented to interrupt the continual demise of the African American community. (The term community is being used as a general term to address the African American population.)

As we take a panoramic view of African American progress since the 60's and through to the beginning of the twenty first century, it is evident that much advancement has taken place. America has African American congresspersons, judges, CEO's of fortune 500 companies, school superintendents, college presidents and professors, leaders of influential organizations, mayors, governors, all kinds of entrepreneurs, sports superstars, Hollywood legends, and in many other places of prominence. African Americans are even represented amongst those who work closely with the President of the United States of America providing advice for the good of all Americans.

Race relations between African and Caucasian Americans are somewhat better than what existed in the past. However, they still require more honest and open dialogue at all levels of society to bring about the kind of harmony and unity that will not tolerate the prejudice and racism that still exists, overtly and covertly, amongst individuals and institutionally. Forgiveness and acceptance are very important concepts necessary to understand and apply in order to witness and experience healing and improvement of relations between the two races.

There are more African American millionaires than America has ever known. Therefore, African Americans are residing in neighborhoods that two generations ago would have been impossible. Many African Americans have "made it" to such a degree that their children's children have no understanding of the hardship that their ancestor's had to experience on a daily basis because of their race. Economically speaking, part of this increase in the economic realm is because many institutions in America are so influenced by "green" (the dollar), that a person's skin color is overlooked. This statement is not to discount the fact that these African Americans have worked hard to reach this level of financial success.

Even in the midst of this undeniable advancement, we see that the African American community is still suffering ills confirming that major problems still exist. AIDS is at an epidemic proportion with an increase amongst African American females. Poverty remains a major issue. As mentioned earlier, there are more African American males in the prison system than any other race. There are more children living in homes without their fathers, often lacking any positive male role model. These and other discrepancies warrant aggressiveness in addressing many issues that the African American family faces to bring about positive changes that will last.

This book is intended to speak to African American marriages and families, to provide a means for internal change. It's purpose is to give the African American community principles and tools that will foster positive change in areas that the family has control over. As the choice is made to implement the biblical principles that are God ordained and that transcend time and ethnicity, I believe that whole neighborhoods will change. Further, even prejudice and racism and shame will have to bow their ugly heads in this land of the free, home of the brave.

As an aside, the tools and principles suggested will help any

American marriage or family that desires to change the course of their generational history, enabling them to receive the blessings that God has awaiting them. Therefore, the suggestions provided are appropriate for all Americans. As you will see in the next few chapters, the information provided can be applied to all levels of society to bring about positive change.

Change, however, does come at a price. It requires time, process, consistency, diligence, and patience in implementing the "new way" of living and relating. There is a saying in the chemical dependency recovery arena that is applicable to anyone or any family desiring positive change. It goes something like this, "to expect positive change by doing the negative things that you have always done, is insanity." Real change requires courage and a decision to do something different. Making changes is probably one of the most difficult actions for anyone or any family when they have become accustomed to a particular style of living and relating. However, as the family keeps their eyes on the prize that these tools and principles can bring about, the implementation becomes an enthusiastic adventure, even though conflict will be encountered at some point along the way.

I am encouraged to see that the government has implemented the African American Healthy Marriage Initiative (AAHMI), an initiative that takes seriously the unfortunate condition of many African American marriages and families, gathering resources to promote positive change. Many other organizations, including churches, have implemented programs, outreaches, or initiatives to serve the African American community in specific areas that are under siege.

It is gratifying to see dialogue and partnerships taking place between African and Caucasian Americans that bring about awareness regarding racial differences. Also, the recognition that these differences are not evil or wrong, but can serve as assets to each other. The place that I believe can have the most authority and influence in bringing positive change for African American families is the Christ-centered/biblically based church as well as Christ-centered/biblically based organizations that are in partnership with the local church.

The local church, especially those in African American

neighborhoods have the potential to effectively implement tools and principles that will enable and empower African American families to "get back what has been lost." That is, our ancestor's sincere dependence on God and commitment to living according to His plan, and accountability to our local churches on an informal and personal level.

It is my hope that African and Caucasian Americans, and any other Americans reading this book, will take the time to digest and pray through the words of this book to hear what the Spirit of the Lord will say to you regarding family life amongst African Americans (and America as a whole). Hopefully, you will be open to how God may guide you into ways in which you can serve as an agent of change in this community that is in dire need of change.

Now that we have a better understanding of the background and issues of African Americans let's turn toward the suggested principles and tools that can be used as an assistant in the goal to see African American families, children and marriages experience improvement rather than the continual demise that we are seeing. These principles and tools appropriately applied will interrupt the negative bringing about positive and lasting change to the African American family and community as a whole.

CHAPTER FIVE

God's Plan for Family Relationships

"Relationships will come and go, but those established with God at the center, will last, will grow and will flow."

Before getting into the meat of our subject, let us take a moment to look at a few words. I firmly believe that we can miss the depth of a sentence or thought because we do not fully understand what all of the words in the sentence mean. Though this may seem elementary, it will help us all to be on one accord.

First word, **God**. Who do you say that He is? Jesus Himself posed this question to the disciples. (Matthew 16:13) Peter, inspired by the Holy Spirit said, *"Thou art the Christ, the Son of the Living God."* (16:16) If we do not first have an accurate understanding of God, who He is, His character, and His plan for mankind, our ability to apply His ways into our lives will be greatly hindered. It is important for you to examine your understanding of God. The Word of God instructs us to examine ourselves.

"Examine yourselves as to whether you are in the faith. Test yourselves. Do you not know yourselves,

that Jesus Christ is in you?— unless indeed you are disqualified."

2 Corinthians 13:5 (NKJ)

As we prayerfully examine ourselves regarding our understanding of God, His Spirit begins to reveal areas of doubt, unbelief, or misunderstanding. As we let go of these, He then reveals His Truth to us in ways that surpass intellectual knowledge and lodge within us; the inner man which is our human spirit. Knowledge that comes by Holy Spirit inspiration is what empowers and enables us to apply God's way into our lives and circumstances with a knowing that God is with us in it. It brings us to a fresher place of believing and walking by faith in God.

We hear many people commenting in our day, that God is who ever or whatever you want him to be. This god is referred to as a Higher Power. Others say that all religions pray to the same God. Then some say that all roads lead to God. It has even been said that we (humans) are gods. The God that we are discussing is the One and Only True God who created all things. (Genesis 1:1, John 1, Mark 12:32, I Corinthians 8:6, Ephesians 4: 5, 6, I Timothy 2:5, Hebrews 11:6)

He came in the flesh as the man, Jesus Christ, and died on the Cross shedding His blood to save us from a sinful lifestyle and eternal damnation. (John 1:14, 3:16) He was resurrected that we might have Life eternal. He operates in the lives of His people by way of His Spirit. (John 14: 16, 17) He is a Triune God. (Genesis 2:26) We come to Him through His Son Jesus Christ. (John 14: 5-7)

As we read the Bible, His Word, we receive revelation from Jesus (who is the Word come in the flesh) about God and His character. As God reveals Himself to us through His Word and prayer, He also heals us of those hurts, attitudes, or beliefs that serve as hindrances to a closer relationship with Him. This relationship is the foundation for all other relationships. The more we get to know God, we get to know ourselves and become more sensitive to others. The more we get to know God, the more freely we flow in His principles, purposes, and plans.

Second word, **Plan.** A plan is a premeditated intentional

purpose. God's plan for mankind came into being before the foundation of the world. (Ephesians 1:4, Hebrews 4:3) It is a plan that is already completed. In Isaiah, we learn that God declares the end to the beginning. (46:10) His plans were established long before we entered into our mother's wombs (Psalm 139:13, Jeremiah 1:5). God continues to watch over us and has sent His Holy Spirit to help in implementing His plan for family life.

Since God is the Creator and created us in His image and likeness, we must believe that He knows what His will, i.e., plan, is for us as families as well as individually. Further that His plan for us is sure and is good, even when circumstances of life look otherwise. (Jeremiah 29:11)

Understanding and accepting that God has a plan for our family life and the success of it brings a level of peace that the world cannot produce. It does not mean we sit back and watch God do His thing. It means that we know that as we do our part, God is steadily at work causing what He premeditated as His intentional purpose for family life, to come to fruition. (Isaiah 46:10, I Thessalonians 5:24) Our part is obedience to His plan.

Our part requires continually going back to the Master (in prayer and meditation) and the Master plan (The Bible) for further revelation, understanding, and instruction. Obedience simply means that wisdom is operating in your life. You are putting God's way into action. Knowing the plan and doing the plan means that your faith in God is intact and that you believe what He says. (James 2:17, John 14:15)

The next word that we want to be sure to understand is the word, **Family**. The Hebrew word for family is *mishpachah*, pronounced mish-paw-khaw. It is defined as *a circle of relatives* and by extension, *a tribe or people.* (Strong's Exhaustive Concordance of the Bible) There are two Greek words for family. "Oikos signifies (a) a dwelling, a house; (b) a household, family, translated 'family' in I Timothy 5:4. (Vine's Expository Dictionary, p.76)

The second Greek word is "patria." It refers primarily to an ancestry or lineage and signifies in the New Testament a family or tribe. It sometimes has a narrow meaning, such as related people and sometimes in a wider sense, of nationalities or races. In

Ephesians 3:15 this Greek word refers to all those who are spiritually related to God the Father. The implication is that those related by blood, biologically or spiritually are considered "family."

Merriam-Webster gives these definitions:

> *group of persons of or regarded as of common ancestry <traditionally all people belong to the family of Noah>*
> *Synonyms: clan, folk, house, kin, kindred, lineage, race, stock, tribe*
> *Related Words: brood, dynasty, line, stirp, strain; issue, offspring, progeny*
> *Idioms: kith and kin, one's own flesh and blood*
>
> *2 a group of usually related persons living in one house and under one head <was the only child in her family>*
> *Synonyms: folks, house, household, and ménage*

Family stems from the word familiar, which implies that family consists of individuals that have some common or familiar aspect that joins them together as one household or tribe or people. One definition in The American Heritage Dictionary is *"a fundamental social group in society consisting especially of a man and woman and their offspring."*

In the beginning after God created man and realized that man was alone, He took female out of man so that the male part of man and female part of man could commune, as two separate entities, together with God. This constitutes the first family. (Genesis 2:18-25) We will discuss this in more detail later. The family as it appears in the beginning was to be a man and a woman in relationship with God. Out of the command of God to be fruitful and multiply, offspring were born. This further intensified the description of "family."

In our society today, the original representation of family, in many cases, does not exist. Though these groups of people living together under the same roof and may not have the man, the woman and the offspring, they are still considered family. The change has come because of man's choice, not God's. God will be near to any family that is near to Him, who are seeking to carry out their lifestyle His way. The point is that the variations that we see today are not what God intended, however are subject to the same spiritual privilege as the originally designed family if they seek relationship with him putting his plan into action.

The final word in our subject is **Relationship**. Relationship refers to how people relate to one another and connotes a level of connectedness or of intimacy. Relationships can be positive or negative. They can be very simplistic to very intense. Usually when relationships are discussed, the reference is to intimate relationships versus the casual.

Family relationships generally fall into the intimate category. Although there are family relationships that are casual, those sharing family life together, especially under the same roof, have developed a peculiar way of relating as a family, which is a form of intimacy. Relationships are very important and essential to our mental, emotional, and spiritual growth. Family relationships shape a child's future relationship choices and modes of relating.

God's desire in the beginning was to have relationship with man. God the Father, The Word, and The Holy Spirit were in relationship with mankind from man's beginning. (John 1:1) Through taking the female out of the man, God desired that the male and female would be in relationship. His ultimate plan was that the man and woman would have relationship together with Him, God the Father, The Word, and The Holy Spirit.

The goal of relationship is sharing, whether it is an event, an activity, a conversation, etc. with another. Ultimately, relationship is sharing lives together. In our discussion we will discuss family relationships; sharing family life. Hopefully, we have a unified understanding of our words. Now, we will discuss God's plan for family relationships.

From the beginning, God's plan for mankind was that man be like Him, to have dominion, and to take authority. The first book of the Bible, Genesis, particularly chapters one through three, gives an account of God's creation of man and His plans for man. In the beginning, God Himself was in relationship. In Genesis 1:26, God

41

says *"let us make man in our own image after our likeness."*

This verse indicates that God was in relationship with others. It speaks of God's triune nature, that of Father, Son, and Holy Spirit. The three have been actively in relationship with each other from the beginning and throughout time. (Example: John 14:16) Then when God made man, He entered into a different kind of relationship. He began relating to His creation.

God is Love. (1 John 4:8) Loves very nature is to express itself to another. God created man that they, Father, Son, and Holy Spirit could express this love to him. God, being a God of relationship desired that man have someone to relate to on his level. That man would have companionship, someone to share in relationship with. Man was in relationship with God, however, although God made man in His image and likeness, man was alone in his realm. When God created man, the Bible says:

> *"So God created man in His own image, in the image of God created He him; male and female created He them." (KJV) Genesis 1:27*

God recognized that though man was in relationship with him and was the dominant creature, that he was alone. He did not like man being alone.

God, in His great love and desire for man to be blessed (to cause to prosper, to bestow blessings on, or a benefit bestowed) decided to make a helper suitable for the man; short for mankind. In man consisted male and female. God in His infinite wisdom took the female part of the man out of the man.

The female part of the man became the helper suitable to the man. "Man" was now male only. The two were once one in the physical. Now God made visible the male and the female. They were still one. God's plan was that this male and this female, the man, remain one in spirit although they were now two physical entities. Without each other they were incomplete, they were not fully man.

The kind of relationship that God established is **Covenant Relationship**. The difference between covenant relationship and other relationships is that covenant carries a lifetime commitment of sharing together. God initiated and entered into covenant with man from the time that He formed him from the dust of the ground. Man broke the covenant with God by engaging in a behavior that was not allowed based on the terms of that covenant.

God had to respond. Every covenant consists of terms of the covenant along with consequences for any departure from the terms. Sacrifice is also a part of a covenant. Although God had to remove man from the garden, because of His great love for mankind, He enacted a plan to restore the covenant relationship that He had with man. The word testament is the same word as the word covenant. In the Old Testament or Covenant God repeatedly entered into covenant with man (Abrahamic, Mosaic, Davidic). The New Testament or Covenant represents the new covenant of God to man through Jesus Christ.

Through the sacrifice of Jesus Christ, i.e., His shedding of blood on the Cross of Calvary, man now had the opportunity to engage in an eternal covenant with Almighty God. This New Covenant has terms as well as consequences. Further, throughout the Old Testament we see man entering into covenant with man. God honors the covenant relationships of His people and expects them to be adhered to. (Joshua 9) When covenants between humans are broken, consequences follow.

The covenant relationship that happens between people consists of the following ingredients:

- Commitment to each other
- A sharing of something of themselves with another
- Each party brings something to the relationship
- There is a sacrifice by each party in entering into the relationship
- Both parties have strengths and weaknesses
- The strengths of one party cover for the weaknesses of the other party and vice versa
- There are terms of agreement and consequences for departure from the terms
- Opportunities to resolve a conflict or reformulate the terms are available

The goal for every Christian should be to learn and understand covenant. The covenant between the individual and God takes place at salvation; man responding in the affirmative to God's plan for eternal relationship. This covenant defines God's terms and man through salvation agrees. It carries with it sacrifice on man's part and consequences when departing from God's terms. This covenant from God's standpoint is everlasting. Any change is man's choice. As long as man continues to follow the terms set forth in God's Word, he is kept safe in the covenant relationship with God.

The covenant made between man to man is best when established based upon God's model for covenant relationship. As such, it carries the same power and resoluteness as the covenant of God to man. In each man is required to work at adhering to the terms of the covenant. When human covenant relationship is understood as a covenant that they have joined with God, the relationship is prone to last because then the goal is to please God as well as man.

A family that is in covenant with each other through the power of God, His Word and the Holy Spirit, are set apart. Not only are their relationships of a different standard than those of the non-Christian, they are also bound together spiritually.

This type of family has great potential in maintaining their family ties and working through difficulties while remaining intact.

Finally, God's ultimate plan for a family that is in covenant with Him is that they be a light to the world, a witness of His love and faithfulness to the non-Christian. The *Family Life* of a family following God's plan for their family becomes a representation of God's way of relationship on earth.

> *Ye are the light of the world. A city that is set on an hill cannot be hid.*
> *Neither do men light a candle, and put it under a bushel, but on a candlestick; and it giveth light unto all that are in the house. Let your light so shine before men, that they may see your good works, and glorify your Father which is in heaven. Matthew 5:14-16*

CHAPTER FIVE

Review

Read each question carefully, then write (T) for true and (F) for false on the line next to the question.

1. _____ Without fully knowing God a family is completely destroyed.

2. _____ A plan is a premeditated intentional purpose.

3. _____ The word "family" has one Greek definition.

4. _____ God was in relationship from the beginning.

5. _____ Covenant relationship with God is an option that we can choose when we become Christians.

6. _____ Scripture clearly states that God is love.

7. _____ Male plus female equals man.

8. _____ God's plan for family life is automatic.

9. _____ Difficulties do not come to a family in covenant with God.

10. _____ God wants His people to be light to the world.

CHAPTER SIX

Family Relationships: Types and Roles

"Order precedes peace"
Bishop B. Courtney McBath

The definition of family and roles that will be presented is based on the biblical perspective of family. That is, The Holy Bible, God's Word to man in written form. The first family is the guideline for God's original intention. A man and one wife, then children born after God Himself declared them husband and wife. The definition of types of family relationships is based upon family units seen in the United States of America.

God's design for family life comes through establishing Divine Order in the home. Order and responsibility must be explained and discussed within the family so that each family member understands, agrees, and adheres to the family rules and boundaries set. The Biblical goal is that each family member accept Jesus Christ as Savior and Lord, therefore will have a greater willingness and desire to walk in righteousness and to please God.

Family Relationship Types

Traditional family - the plan from the beginning of time was that a man and a woman who were in relationship with God and were committed to one another as husband and wife, would come together in sexual union to produce children. In order to rear their children adequately, it would be necessary for the mother to do her part and the father to do his part. This would help the children to learn and grow into healthy maturity so when they became adults, they would know and understand how to respond to their spouse and how to rear their children.

An **extended family** generally consists of a mother and father along with their children and other adult family members who share the responsibility of caring for the children. It can also consist of grandparents, aunts, uncles and cousins sharing together in family relationship.

A **blended family (or step-family)** is a family that consists of one biological parent and their spouse and children of either or both spouses.

A **single parent family** consists of one parent (male or female) and their biological or adopted child or children.

The description of a **Biblical family** begins when a man and a woman enter into a marital relationship. They consummate their marriage eventually giving birth to children. The addition of children intensifies the family relationship making the family a family. In our society, a family, in some cases, begins out of wedlock, meaning that the child is born into a single parent family and/or a joint custody arrangement wherein the children are required to live with each parent a specified amount of time throughout the month. In other cases, a breakup of a living together arrangement or a divorce causes a family crisis and adjustment requiring a custody decision and visitation arrangement. Some children are living with their grandparents, other relatives or close family friends due to a variety of reasons.

Regardless as to the family type, children need parents or parental figures in order to grow healthy physically, emotionally, mentally, and spiritually. Husband and wife need each other because without the other they are incomplete in their oneness in

Christ and unable to fully carry out their God given responsibilities. In single parent families, the adult and child (or children) need a support system to aid them in proper growth and development and to have an outlet to prevent stress and family conflict.

Family Roles

The role of the husband is:
- Love his wife as his own body and as Christ loves the church and gave Himself up for her
- Sacrifice himself for his wife
- To provide, protect, and serve as spiritual leader for his wife
- To be gentle with his wife
- To pray for and with his wife
- Seek to understand his wife being sensitive to her femininity
- Sharing the grace of life together as partners
- Manage his household

(Scriptural References: Genesis 2:24, Colossians 3:19, Ephesians 5:25-28, I Peter 3:7, I Timothy 3:5, I Timothy 5:8)

The role of the wife is:
- To be helper/partner to her husband in fulfilling the challenges of life
- To directly and indirectly assist him
- To encourage her husband and to pray for and with him
- To respect her husband
- To assist her husband in household management
- To submit to her own husband

(Scriptural References: Genesis 2:20b, Ephesians 5:22-24, Proverbs 31: 11-12, I Peter 3:1-6)

The father's role is:
- The main provider and protector
- The director of the family

- Shares in nurturing and caretaker for children
- Spends time with children instructing them in the way of righteousness
- Is to be sensitive to the emotional needs of his children

(Scriptural References: Dueteronomy 6:6-7, 11:19, Ephesians 6:4, I Timothy 5:8, Proverbs 6:20, 22:6,18)

The mother's role is:
- The main nurturer and caretaker for children
- She joins with her husband in directing their family
- Spends time with children instructing them in the way of righteousness
- To serve as household manager

(Scriptural References: Dueteronomy 6:6-7, 11:19, Proverbs 6:20, 22:6,18, 31: 27-28)

The role of both parents is:
- to care for the child (or children) in every way that the child needs caring in order to grow each stage of life on into adulthood, normal and healthy
- Model biblical behavior in their attitude, actions, and speech, i.e., practice the presence of Jesus
- To diligently pray for and with their children
- To assist their children in growing in the knowledge of God and in their personal relationship with the Lord

(Scriptural References: Dueteronomy 6:6-7, 11:19, Proverbs 22:6,18)

The role of the stepparent is:
- To stand alongside the biological parent in the rearing of their children
- Same role responsibilities as those listed above depending upon the specific needs of the family (using wisdom when disciplining the step child)

(Scriptural References: Dueteronomy 6:6-7, 11:19, Proverbs 22:6,18)

The role of <u>children</u> is:
- to respect, honor and obey their parents with the unspoken understanding that their parents love them and are looking out for their best interest

(Scriptural References: Exodus 20:12, Deuteronomy 5:16, Proverbs 1:8, 6:20, Ephesians 6:1-3, Colossians 3:20)

The role of a <u>family</u> is:
- To support, encourage and help one another
- To accept one another without conditions
- to confront one another when one places themselves in a harmful or destructive situation
- to submit to and respect one another

(Scriptural References: I Peter 3:8, Ephesians 5:21)

Note: See Appendix III for Scriptural References noted above

Many books have been written and research conducted to discuss or determine the effects of parent's roles on their children's lives and/or emotional development. Parents have an overwhelming influence on the molding of their children. Their attitudes and behaviors can either make or break their child. Following are some emotional qualities that a child receives when in engaging in a positive (not perfect) parent/child relationship.

What Children Receive From Parents:

Father:

- *identity*
- *esteem for self*
- *stability*
- *sense of security*
- *feeling protected*
- *provided for*
- *how to (or not to) relate to the opposite sex*

Fathers help children have a sense of knowing that they have the ability to make it in life.

Mother:
- *sense of belonging*
- *feeling wanted*
- *feeling loved and cared for*
- *a sense of worth and value*
- *feeling understood*
- *nurturing*
- *how to (or not to) relate to the opposite sex*

Mothers help children learn how to develop intimacy/closeness with others.

When children do not have the proper bonding and intimacy with both parents, it causes:

- *problems of identity*
- *low self-esteem*
- *depression*
- *rebellion*
- *criminal behaviors*
- *feelings of rejection or abandonment*
- *poor relationship management*
- *vulnerability to harmful/abusive treatment by others*

Note: See Appendices IV & V For Parenting Tips

MAIN RESPONSIBILITIES OF PARENTS

- *Nurture:* to provide loving and caring attention; cultivate; nourish
  (Deuteronomy 6:6,7)

- *Teach:* giving instruction on life and basic skills, including biblical morals and values
  (Deuteronomy 6:6,7; Proverbs 22:6,18)

- *Love:* speaks of affection, attitude, and action
  (I Corinthians 13:4-8)

- *Discipline:* a systematic method to obtain obedience, includes love [teaching child how to behave with respect for self and others]
  (Proverbs 22:15; Hebrews 12:5-11; Proverbs 23:13, 14)

- *Modeling:* serving as an example in action and in what you believe and teach
  (I Timothy 2:15)

- *Provide:* making appropriate plans to meet continued and future basic physical and other needs
  (I Timothy 5:8)

- **_Protect_**: to defend against harm or danger and to remove from potential harm or danger
  (I Corinthians 13:7)

(*Main Responsibilities of Parents* qualities noted are from an unidentified author)

> **"When parents do what is right, they help keep their child from doing what is wrong."**

BIBLICAL ROLES VERSUS SPIRITUAL GIFTINGS AND CALLINGS

Biblical roles in marriage and the family have often been confused causing conflict and division in family relationships. Further, Biblical roles in marriage and family have often been confused with **spiritual gifting and callings** causing great controversy amongst spouses as well as in the family of God, i.e., the Body of Christ.

As we are admonished in Proverbs 4:7 "...*in all thy getting, get understanding.*" The more that we understand God's love, ways and commands, the more that we can flow in God's order and peace in our relationships. (Proverbs 3:13)

I Corinthians 14:40 tells us to "...*let all things be done in decency and in order.*" (KJV) - God is a God of decency and order.

Biblical Order has to do with God's way of doing things, with obedience and fulfilling the covenant requirements. Submission to God's way keeps the covenant relationship intact and the power of God activated in your marriage and family relationships. (I Chronicles 15:13)

> **_Galatians 3:28-29_** says "*There is neither Jew nor Greek, there is neither bond nor free, there is neither male nor female: for ye are all one in Christ Jesus. And if ye be Christ's, then are ye Abraham's seed, and heirs according to the promise.*" (KJV)

Spiritual Gifting and Calling have to do with fulfilling the destiny, plan, or purpose that God has for your life in order to advance His Kingdom. It could, at times, simply have to do with accomplishing specific assignments that He has given you that will in some way advance His Kingdom on earth. (I Corinthians 12:11, Romans 12:6)

I Corinthians 13:1-3 talks about walking in God's love.

> *If I speak in the tongues of men and of angels, but have not love, I am only a resounding gong or a clanging cymbal. If I have the gift of prophecy and can fathom all mysteries and all knowledge, and if I have a faith that can move mountains, but have not love, I am nothing.* (NIV)

Both our Biblical role and spiritual gifts or call require that we operate in the humility and love of God. The description of The Fruit of the Spirit (Galatians 5:22) and the Love passage (I Corinthians 13:4-8), along with other Biblical passages, help us to operate in the humility and love of God. *This is a choice that each person must make.* Yielding to the Love of God as we submit to His roles and rules better enables us to be the *Light of the world.* We are then better able to accomplish His purposes with balance, which is provided by the Spirit of God. The Holy Spirit gives direction and instruction specific to our situations, which are always in line with God's Word.

One of the reasons that I chose to mention the difference between biblical roles and spiritual gifts and callings is to address the problems that many families experience as they begin to walk in their gifts or call. I have seen situations in which women who are wives and mothers, begin to exalt their spiritual gifts or call above their role and responsibility to their husbands and children. Some of these women chose divorce when their husbands would not get in line with their spiritual gifts or call.

Also, many men have taken on the work of ministry as if it were their other woman and the people they minister to, as their children, while leaving little time to provide the ministry that their wives and children need from them. All of this counts as disorder and is a deceit from the enemy of our relationships. It is a subtle attempt to keep Christians from being the light to the world that God created us to be.

If we lack understanding about God's order and the purpose for this order, we enter a cycle of disorder that leads to marriage and family chaos. Biblical roles and spiritual gifts and callings should never be in conflict. God made us. He knows His plans for every living being, each individual person. God is not the author of confusion. He would not set you in a biblical role, then decide to confuse you with a spiritual gift or call that will interfere with or interrupt your biblical role.

When operated in the Love of God and led by His Holy Spirit, our roles, gifts and calls will compliment one another. The problem that many people tend to experience is waiting on the timing and way that God wants to implement the gifts and call. Or, perhaps, the gifts and call are in operation in a way and at a level that has not been recognized or understood because it may not be a visible or traditional religious activity.

As we honor God with the whole of our lives, particularly, as we willingly with joy, submit to the responsibilities of our biblical roles, we will experience the blessing of more opportunity to operate in the spiritual gifts and call in a way that enhances family life rather than takes away from it.

Husbands must accept that God's gifts or call on their wives life is a compliment to them as her husband. As you embrace and support her, your relationship is enhanced and grows deeper, that is when proper order and balance are at work. You will find yourself at "the city gate," a place of honor because of this wife that God has blessed you with.

Wives must realize and accept that when God has placed a ministry burden on her husband's life, as his helpmeet, wife, you are expected to help him fulfill the assignment, spiritual gift or call that God has placed on his life. God calling your husband is a testimony of what God thinks of you as his wife. He has entrusted you with a precious gift.

Often one spouse may be jealous of the other. This means that covenant is not understood and/or communication and love are not properly operating in your relationship. The mere conflict indicates that there is a need to bring the issue before God to get His view of the matter as well as His solution. God made us for peace. When there is no peace, there is disorder at work and wrong choices being made. Romans 12:18 states "if possible, so far as it depends on you, be at peace with all men." All men certainly includes a husband and wife.

To operate in a spiritual gift or call and not have peace in the relationships that mean the most is a discrepancy. This in itself leaves room for the devil to get a foothold. Operating in God's order, i.e., biblical roles must be our priority. This is what proves to the world that we are made in the image and likeness of God. The way that we carry out our family relationships says to the world that we are a chosen people and that we love our God. The work of ministry, the formal or traditional means of expressing our spiritual gifts or call are secondary to carrying out our biblical roles and relationships with our family members.

If we cannot implement biblical principles in our homes and with the people that we love, our attempts to do so with others are hypocritical. This doesn't mean that marriages or families never have a disagreement or a conflict between a role responsibility and a responsibility of the call. What it does mean is that application of the word of God in all situations will bring us to a God solution, which brings peace, even if it takes a while. We must be willing to battle for our family relationships, walking in the roles that God instituted allowing God, by His Spirit to arrange and cause His plans regarding our gifts and call to flow forth in His timing and in His way. He is the One who created us. He has all the answers and knows what he has in store for each one of us. Our relationship with Him enables us to get the information from Him and access His peace. Letting God have the charge of our lives will allow us to experience a fuller marriage and family life than what we ourselves can arrange.

CHAPTER SIX

Review

Name: _____
Class: _____
Period: _____
Date: _____

Read each question carefully, then write (T) for true and (F) for false on the line next to the question.

1. _____ Order and responsibility in the family must be explained (understood) in order to be effective.

2. _____ The Biblical perspective of family life is important only for some Christian families.

3. _____ There are at least four family relationship types in America.

4. _____ Regardless, of the family type or make-up, children do not need parents to grow healthy; physically, mentally, emotionally, and spiritually.

5. _____ God has given instruction in the Bible about family roles & responsibilities.

6. _____ Children receive the same mental and emotional compensations from mother and father.

7. _____ Step-parents have no responsibilities regarding their stepchildren.

8. _____ Parents have at least five responsibilities to fulfill according to God's standards for family life.

9. _____ Fathers help children to have the sense of knowing that they have the ability to make it in life.

10. _____ Mothers help children to learn how to develop intimacy/closeness with others.

Bonus Question: What is the difference between Biblical roles and spiritual gifts or call?

CHAPTER SEVEN

Family Enhancers (Part 1)

"Even if it ain't broke, every family can use some fixin"

Following are suggested aids to enhance your family life, relationships, and prosperity. It is important to implement the aids that will add to your family allowing you to experience God's best and blessing for you, causing your family to bring the glory to God that is due Him. Hopefully, these suggested aids will help your family stop negative patterns of relating and bring in a fresh new atmosphere into your household.

Breaking Generational Curses

Many families have recognizable patterns of behavior or speech, and sometimes attitudes that tend to be particular to the members of their family. Some of these behaviors, speech or attitudes are of no concern, just peculiar to the particular family. Some come about through learned behaviors that are imparted through continued experience (modeling) or because of the environment that the family members become accustomed to.

However, some behaviors, speech or attitudes are of great concern because of their destructiveness to the individual, relationships and to family growth, security and stability. Any behaviors, speech, or attitudes that serve to bring destruction to the family, or that steal or kill aspects of good family relationship is not of or from God and need to be addressed.

The Bible clearly states:

> *The thief cometh not, but for to steal, and to kill, and to destroy: I am come that they might have life, and that they might have it more abundantly. John 10:10 (KJV)*

God's desire, through sending His Son, Jesus Christ to die as a sacrifice for us was that we would no longer be bent toward sinfulness but that we would have *Life* and have it in abundance. This Life that Jesus brings us does not steal from us, kill us, or destroy us. The one who does this, known as the thief, is Satan, called also the devil. His aim, his very job, his purpose, his intent, his plan, is to steal from, kill, and destroy mankind. He will attempt to accomplish his purpose by any means necessary.

One of the ways that Satan has had some success in destroying families is through generational curses. These are behaviors, speech, or attitudes that are destructive to the individual or family and are of a spiritual nature although they operate in the physical realm. Chester and Betsy Kylstra of Proclaiming His Word, Inc. use the term, *"Sins of the Fathers and Resulting Curses,"* in their Restoring the Foundations ministry. They suggest that we are often set up for problems because of the past sins of our ancestors (family members) that become curses. We then engage in self-sins that continue to negatively affect our family line.

The sins of the fathers and resulting curses must be dealt with in order for us to actually walk in the abundant Life that Christ has provided for us. One mistake that many Christians make is believing that once we enter salvation that everything is taken care of and we are okay. The truth is that our walk with Christ is a life of sanctification, which includes an ongoing getting rid of any and everything that hinders our life in Christ. Generational curses are often ignored and not seen for what they really are and become accepted as a way of life, something that just is.

As believers in Christ Jesus, we have a power working with us and within us that is greater *"...than he that is in the world."* (I John 4:4) In order to better enhance our family relationships and family success, it is important to consider breaking generational curses that may be in operation.

Examples of sins of the fathers and resulting curses (generational curses) are:

- <u>Addictive or Compulsive Behaviors</u> - alcoholism, workaholism, drug addiction, eating disorders, etc.
- <u>Sexual Sins</u> - fornication, adultery, pornography, sexual abuse, masturbation, sexual addictions, etc.
- <u>Occult</u> - witchcraft, voodoo, astrology, sorcery, fortune telling, white magic, black magic, etc.
- <u>Sickness/Diseases</u> - including mental illness, physical abnormalities, premature death, etc.
- <u>Emotional problems</u> - fear, shame, anger, bitterness, rejection, violence, hostility, depression, etc.
- <u>Financial Bondage</u> - poverty, debt, greediness, stinginess, undisciplined spending, robbing God, etc.
- <u>Idolatry</u> - social status, (idolizing) worship of man, position, possessions, ministry, etc.
- <u>Relationship Problems</u> - separation, divorce, division, unfaithfulness, out of wedlock births, conflict, contention, disrespectful, inability to love or express love, criticalness, etc.
- <u>Religious Bondage</u> - man made doctrines, legalism, cults, false religions (secret societies including masons, fraternities, sororities), hypocrisy, etc.
- <u>Rebellion or Stubbornness</u> - pride, disobedience, defiance, jealousy, envy
- <u>Ungodly Speech</u> - cursing, profanity, strife, blaming, gossip, defaming others, etc.
- <u>Unlawful Behavior</u> - lying, stealing, cheating, illegal business pursuits, tax evasion, etc.

From: <u>Restoring the Foundations: Counseling by the Living Word</u>, Chester & Betsy Kylstra, Proclaimimg His Word, Inc., PO Box 2339, Santa Rosa Beach, FL, 1996

These sins of the fathers and resulting curses or generational curses can be broken through repentance, forgiveness, renouncing, and acceptance of God's way of doing things putting them into action. The first step, however, is the step that is difficult for many people because of pride or shame. This step requires acknowledging the sins or curses. Bishop T.D. Jakes has a teaching entitled *"Admit it, Quit it and Forget it."* He expresses that admitting a sin is the first step toward honestly dealing with it.

Once we can admit and acknowledge the problems, sins, or issues that cause destruction, whether major or minor, we are better able "to quit it and forget it." That is, no longer allowing that thing the control over our lives and relationships that it once had. At this point, we have broken the power of the enemy in the spiritual realm. This is taking the authority that we have as believers in Christ Jesus. This allows a person or family to be in the position that from the beginning God desired for mankind; to have dominion. After confessing, forgiving, repenting, renouncing and breaking Satan's power "through the redemptive work of Christ on the Cross and His shed blood", putting this change in to action is a process.

This is a process that entails changing and renouncing the belief system that may have come about as a result of these generational curses. The belief system is not always on the conscious level so requires brutal honesty in dealing with what we believe about specific issues, situations, relationships, etc. It is necessary to accept what the Word of God says regarding these concerns.

Dealing with the deep or hidden hurts and/or wounds of the soul that may have come because of these generational curses is important to maintaining the legal ground that has been regained. Finally, demonic oppression may need to be addressed so the individual or family is free of the spiritual influences that have become familiar to them ensuring that they no longer have that opportunity.

Lastly, through understanding that we are soldiers in the army of Lord, and therefore in a spiritual battle in which we already have the victory, fighting for our family life is less of a burden and understood as a necessity to maintaining the victory gained.

God's Love and The Five Love Languages

As mentioned earlier, <u>our God is a God of love</u>. Actually, the Bible states *"God is love."* (I John 4:8) The kind of love that is exhibited by God is *agape* love. This is an unconditional love. He loves us without condition. This is demonstrated by the fact that He sent His Son to die for us while we were still in a sinful state. (Romans 5:8) Further, God made this provision for us before we were even born, although He had us in mind. (Jeremiah 1:5, Psalms 139:16)

Some say that the Cross of Jesus represents God's love to man and man's love to God (vertically) and man's love to man (horizontally). That God is as concerned about us loving Him as He is about us loving one another. Jesus stated that to love our neighbor was the second commandment after loving God with all our heart, soul, and mind. (Mark 12:31) Jesus Himself instructs us, to love others the way he loves us.

> *A new commandment I give unto you, That ye love one another; as I have loved you, that ye also love one another. By this shall all men know that ye are my disciples, if ye have love one to another. John 13:34-35 (KJV)*

Later in the Scripture, we are told that if we profess to love God but hate our brother than our love is not real. There is no in between. Either we love or we hate. Some Christians sometime jokingly say, " I have to love you, but I don't have to like you." That statement does not agree with God's way of love. Those that say this justify their attitude by saying, "we are not commanded to like." However, God's love goes beyond the natural feelings and attitudes and yields itself to God and His way of loving. In other words, rather than operating in the flesh (the sinful nature), we choose to operate, that is, live by the Spirit. (Romans 8: 4-14, Galatians 5: 13-18, 25)

> *If a man say, I love God, and hateth his brother, he is*

a liar: for he that loveth not his brother whom he hath seen, how can he love God whom he hath not seen? And this commandment have we from him, That he who loveth God love his brother also. I John 4:20-21 (KJV)

Loving others the way God loves comes through loving God and making a decision to be obedient to His command. The Holy Spirit helps us to carry out our act of obedience and gives us the ability to love even the unlovable (such as our enemies). When we make the choice to love, eventually we begin to feel differently about the person because God imparts within us the emotion that goes along with that act.

Gary Chapman wrote a profound bestseller entitled The Five Love Languages. In it, he discusses five primary love languages. He suggests that there is a primary way in which every individual feels loved. It is not based on how we want to love that person or what we think we should do to express our love. It is based solely on what makes that person feel loved. He taps into God's way of loving by suggesting that we take the time to learn what our loved ones love language is, then begin to love them in that way.

Choosing to love God's way takes the focus off self and puts the focus upon the one we love. Loving this way is giving. The late Dr. Edwin Louis Cole of Christian Men's Network, in describing God's way of love versus lust, states, *"Love gives at the expense of self to benefit others while lust takes at the expense of others to benefit self."* God's promise to us is that as we give it shall be given unto us in good measure. Also, that we will reap whatever we sow. Further that we are not to give up in sowing good things, but as we continue to do the righteous thing, we will eventually reap. Often the following verses are mentioned when discussing the giving of money, however, the emphasis is that of giving.

Give, and it shall be given unto you; good measure, pressed down, and shaken together, and running over, shall men give into your bosom. For with the same measure that ye mete withal it shall be measured to you again. Luke 6:38 (KJV)

Be not deceived; God is not mocked: for whatsoever a man soweth, that shall he also reap. For he that soweth to his flesh shall of the flesh reap corruption; but he that soweth to the Spirit shall of the Spirit reap life everlasting. And let us not be weary in well doing: for in due season we shall reap, if we faint not. Galatians 6:7-9 (KJV)

But this I say, He which soweth sparingly shall reap also sparingly; and he which soweth bountifully shall reap also bountifully. Every man according as he purposeth in his heart, so let him give; not grudgingly, or of necessity: for God loveth a cheerful giver. 2 Corinthians 9:6-7 (KJV)

The emphasis here is to choose to express love to your family members in the ways that please them and you will notice that at some point you begin to reap love; loving acts that please you. (Proverbs 11:25)

The Five Love Languages are as follows:

- Love Language #1: <u>Words of Affirmation</u>

- Love Language #2: <u>Quality Time</u>

- Love Language # 3: <u>Receiving Gifts</u>

- Love Language # 4: <u>Acts of Service</u>

- Love Language # 5: <u>Physical Touch</u>

From: Gary Chapman, The Five Love Languages, Northfield Publishing, Chicago, IL, 1992. ISBN:1-881273-15-6

If appropriate, as a suggestion, your family could use the five languages as a family discussion with each member identifying their primary love language. This, along with prayer and understanding God's love can help to bring about a new sense of care and concern for one another and invite a spirit of love into your home.

CHAPTER EIGHT

Family Enhancers (Part 2)

"Just a little more fixin' to make it good"

Family Devotion/Bible Study, Fun Time, Meetings, and Family Sabbath

Family Life will greatly improve through the entrance of God's Word. There is a power in the Word of God that is almost indescribable. When family members share Gods' Word together and put it into practice in the home, that home becomes a lighthouse to others. The Word of God washes and cleanses and adds joy and peace to the household.

Regardless as to the ages represented in your home, you can incorporate a **Family Devotion or Bible Study**. Most Christian bookstores have Bible study or devotional books on their shelves for every age and level. They range from the traditional type to the creative. The important ingredients are the family coming together around God's Word and choosing to put into action what is learned or discussed.

Family Fun Time is a time when the family chooses to engage together in some leisure activity. This can range from no cost to great cost. It can be in the home or out of the home. Some activities can be playing a board game, singing songs together, watching a comedy, making use of a book with suggested activities, to enjoying a play together or going away on a camping trip or a vacation. The important aspect of Family Fun Time is that the family shares in a fun activity with each other. The fun time together reduces stress and adds a joyfulness and deeper sense of intimacy to the family that is consistent in sharing time together.

Family Meetings help to enhance family relationships by allowing for a time when family members can openly and honestly discuss issues of concern in a spirit of love. The family can together discuss options to resolving the issues in a way that is best for the family and will add to the family cohesiveness. These meetings can also be used as a time to inform the family of changes in schedules, about upcoming events or activities or for the sharing of any information that will have impact on the family.

The fourth commandment of the Ten Commandments is about the **Sabbath**. We are commanded to *"remember the sabbath and to keep it holy."* (Exodus 20:8) The Sabbath is one day out of seven that we are to set aside in observance of the Lord. It is a day that God gives us to rest and remember Him. Work is not to done on this day. It is a day of shutting down the normal activities and focusing our time and attention on God. As I studied the Sabbath, I learned that this is to be a family day. The whole family is to observe the Sabbath.

> *Remember the sabbath day, to keep it holy. Six days shalt thou labour, and do all thy work:*
> *But the seventh day is the sabbath of the LORD thy God: in it thou shalt not do any work, thou, nor thy son, nor thy daughter, thy manservant, nor thy maidservant, nor thy cattle, nor thy stranger that is within thy gates: For in six days the LORD made heaven and earth, the sea, and all that in them is, and rested the seventh day: wherefore the LORD blessed the sabbath day, and hallowed it.*
> *Exodus 20:8-11 (KJV)*

Our contemporary society is so busy and has a difficult time understanding rest. Attempting to set aside a whole day, for some families, is unthinkable. However, I believe that as we make a family decision to incorporate the Sabbath into our Family Life, we will see results of a supernatural nature.

To make this day less cumbersome, the day that your family spends in worship with other saints (church) could be the day that the family chooses to shut down and focus on the Lord. After church service, the family can share a meal together at which time a prayer and a discussion about the Lord can be included. Perhaps, the family can discuss a new way that they have experienced the Lord that week or how knowing God impacted a situation that week. Focusing on a characteristic or name of God is another way to keep God as the focus.

We are blessed with Christian television. On that day that your family chooses to observe the Sabbath, you can watch Christian television or a Christian video rather than viewing secular television or videos. Another option is to engage in Bible based games or reading a Christian novel or another type of Christ centered book. Even a family study about the Sabbath can be used as a means to help the family understand what the Sabbath is, why God commanded it, implications for contemporary Christians, and how it can be observed. As we mentioned earlier in this writing, ignorance is often the cause of problems in our family life. Incorporating this command, with understanding, will without doubt bring greater blessing into your Family Life. The emphasis is receiving the rest (spiritual & natural), as a family, that God has provided for His children.

Another means to enhancing family life is in **developing family communication skills**. Lack of communication amongst family members is the cause of unnecessary conflict and can lead to a devastating breakdown in the family. When conflicts arise, the family must be willing to loving deal with the conflict at hand to keep it from bringing division within the family. The biblical directive to handling conflict is that we be reconciled with the other person through addressing offenses by speaking the truth in love and forgiving one another. (Matthew 5:23, Mark 11:25, Ephesians 4:25). By doing this we give no place to the devil in our family life. (Ephesians 4:26, 27)

In the book, <u>Caring Enough to Confront</u> by David Augsburger, the term *"care-fronting"* is introduced. He suggests that confrontations should take place between people who care about one another, however should be done with care. You care, yet you need to confront. Care-fronting is an alternative to maintaining relationships by confronting in a caring way, thus making the relationship even better.

Care-fronting entails:

- offering genuine caring that bids another to grow
- unites love and power
- unifies concern for relationship with concern for goals
- a way to communicate with both impact and respect, with truth and love
- has a unique view of conflict

5 Options to conflict:

1. I'll get him/her - I win, you lose
2. I'll get out - I want out, I'll withdrawal
3. I'll give in - I'll give in for good relations
4. I'll meet halfway
5. I care enough to confront - I love you and want this relationship to work, I want us both to grow/to benefit (win/win)

Important aspects of care-fronting:

- Listening
- Speaking
- Honesty
- Making statements
- Asking a clear question
- Limiting complaints
- Willing to talk it out nicely
- Expressing anger in a non-destructive manner

From: **CARING ENOUGH TO CONFRONT: How to Understand and Express Our Deepest Feelings Toward Others, David Augsburger, Herald Press, 1973**

Important to good family communication is <u>fair fighting versus dirty fighting</u>. Dirty fighting (see Appendix VI) is destructive and eventually leads to family division. Fair fighting means that the family agrees to respect one another, listen to hear one another, avoids dirty fighting at all costs and works toward positive resolve of family problems.

Learning and incorporating <u>communication techniques</u> into the family can serve as tools to opening the channels of communication and help to bring a freedom and openness to the family that can enhance family intimacy. Many churches, ministries and counseling organizations present training and seminars to help build lasting relationships through techniques that assist in bringing about honest and open communication between loved ones.

Bookstores and libraries are filled with self-help books addressing building family intimacy. Christian counselors are available to assist a family in learning and incorporating communication techniques into their family life that can help to improve relationships.* The family must be willing. Even willing yourselves to be willing can be blessed by God and lead your family into more productive ways of relating. (See James 1:19,20)

Effective Communication includes:

- Eye contact
- Attentive body language
- Appropriate vocal qualities
- Active listening
- Empathy
- Probing

From: Collins, Gary R., <u>How to be a People Helper,</u> Tyndale House Publishers, 1995.

*BAACC (Black African American Christian Counselors) is a good resource for referrals to Christian counselors who provide counseling for African Americans (www.aacc.net, then click the link to BAACC).

It is important that family communication is clearly understood by all members. Therefore, it is necessary to ascertain whether the other person understood what you said the way you meant it. There are actually six messages that come through in a conversation:

1. What you mean to say
2. What you actually say
3. What the other person hears you say
4. What the other person thinks he hears
5. What the other person says about what you said
6. What you think the other person said about what you said

From: Wright, H. Norman, <u>Communication: The Key to Your Marriage,</u> Regal Books. 1974

Family members must choose to be compassionate with one another. We all make mistakes and will sometimes blunder in our understanding of each other. Love, however, will take the time to clarify rather than expect that the other person automatically understands, or is a mind reader, or heard what you said the way you meant it. Applying basic communication skills and techniques will enhance your family life turning the negative and unhealthy ways of communicating into positive and healthy ways.

CHAPTERS SEVEN & EIGHT

Review

Name: _____
Class: _____
Period: _____
Date: _____

Read each question carefully, then print the letter of the correct answer on the line next to the question.

1. _____ **Family enhancers are**
    a. Improving communication between spouses only.
    b. Suggested aids to enhance family life.
    c. Not necessary.

2. _____ **Breaking generational curses**
    a. Allows a family to take back legal ground that Satan has stolen.
    b. Only affects attitudes.
    c. Is accomplished through forgiveness.

3. _____ **The Greek word for God's love is**
    a. Storge
    b. Phileo
    c. Agape

4. _____ **A love language**
    a. Is foreign language, like Spanish.
    b. The way two people in love talk to each other.
    c. A primary way in which every individual feels loved.

5. _____ The five love languages are
    a. kissing, holding hands, going on a date, engagement, marriage
    b. Words of affirmation, quality time, receiving gifts, acts of service, physical touch.
    c. Spanish, Greek, Latin, French, Hebrew.

6. _____ God's Word if followed
    a. Can improve family life
    b. Won't necessarily improve family life
    c. Improves family life

7. _____ Spending time with family
    a. Is very important to family intimacy.
    b. Is a good thing to do if you have the time.
    c. Doesn't really matter.

8. _____ The Sabbath is
    a. Something that only the Jews engaged in.
    b. The fourth of the Ten Commandments.
    c. Is a day of sleeping and watching movies.

9. _____ Care-fronting is
    a. an alternative to maintaining relationships by confronting in a caring way.
    b. Allows you to win the argument.
    c. Is only for marriages.

10. _____ Family communication is effective when
    a. Clearly understood by all family members.
    b. The family engages in proper eye contact.
    c. Dirty fighting is at a minimal.

Godly Family Financial Planning

"It is the love of money, (not money itself),
that is the root of all evil"
I Timothy 6:10

God has made us stewards of our lives and all that concerns us. Stewardship indicates that the owner has left someone else in charge of his possessions and is allowing them to use his possessions as if they belong to the stewards, i.e., to benefit from what he has left. Good stewardship warrants that we have knowledge of the owner's rules, regulations, and/or peculiarities in how he would prefer that his possessions be managed.

To manage his possessions according to personal likes, dislikes and preferences could cause a person to stray far from what the owner desires and put the person in jeopardy of losing the benefits entrusted to him. It could also cause the person much hardship when operating out of the boundaries set by the owner. There are consequences to mismanaging that one cannot avoid. Doing the right thing with what has been entrusted brings forth benefits, rewards, and continued prosperity. Mismanaging brings forth demise, destruction and eventual failure to produce.

Stewardship involves a level of trust and belief in the owner. A person is able to accept the stewardship requirements because in their estimation, the owner has credibility. It is understood that he knows more than the steward does and that the owner's requirements are for the steward's good. The stewards can trust that the owner's goal is to watch over his possessions bringing benefits and prosperity to those stewards who engage in his requirements. It is further understood that the owner has the necessary knowledge to provide the wisdom and instruction needed in order to give the stewards guidance in good stewardship.

Our lives are not our own. They belong to God. God, in His great love for us, allows us the opportunity to exert our will, to choose to be the kind of stewards that he desires us to be. This is our choice. It is a choice of obedience versus disobedience. Obeying God's requirements for the good stewardship of every aspect of our lives is considered an act of faith in God and living in a godly manner.

When it comes to finances, we tend to think that it is up to us to determine how they are to be used. As understanding comes about tithing and the responsibility of every Christian to engage in this aspect of worship to God, many Christians begin to tithe. However, research shows that only a small percentage of American Christians tithe. Many still believe that tithing is an option. Others believe that they have a right to refuse to tithe because they do not trust the men, i.e., those that run the church.

God tells us in Deuteronomy 12 that He will show us where He would have us worship. That the place He shows us is the place where we are to bring our tithes. (vs. 5-8) He admonishes us to be careful not to give our tithes and offerings anywhere we please. (vs. 12, 13)

The truth concerning finances is that 100% of our finances belong to God. He wants us to exhibit good stewardship over all 100%. We know that the first 10% of our finances is definitely a tithe to the Lord. We tend to think that the remaining 90% are ours to do with them as we wish. God through Matthew 6:33 instructs us to " seek first the Kingdom of God and His righteousness.

He wants us to understand how His Kingdom operates in order for us to be good stewards of our lives and the possessions that he entrusts to us. God expects us to handle our family finances according to His design. Once we do this, our obedience to Him leads us to the blessings that God wants us to have. These blessings are God's care for us and the manifestation of His promise noted in Matthew 13:11-12,

> *He answered and said to them, "Because it has been given to you to know the mysteries of the kingdom of heaven, but to them it has not been given. For whoever has, to him more will be given, and he will have abundance; but whoever does not have, even what he has will be taken away from him." (NKJ)*

God wants us to understand the mysteries of His Kingdom. The more understanding that we have, the more we will apply Kingdom principles to our lives, and the more God blesses us. I heard a minister say that as we seek to know God and His Word, we begin to discover how God thinks. Eventually, we begin to think like God as we encounter the situations of this life. God's care for us goes far beyond the 100% that he has entrusted to us.

Deuteronomy 8: 18 informs us that God has given us the ability to get wealth. Wealth covers the whole spectrum of what life consists of: money, resources, power, land, strength, goods, riches, substance, etc. God wants His people to be well provided for. His expectation is that wealth turns us towards Him in thanksgiving, praise and a deeper commitment to Him, rather than arrogance and self-sufficiency.

The wealth that God intends is accompanied by peace and joy and comes through our obedience to God's commands. His commands are not optional. We are not to meet our own needs. God meets our needs (Philippians 4:13) and our obedience to His commands initiates our needs being met. God, however goes beyond our needs and brings wealth to our families.

Christians are disciples of Jesus Christ, AKA, The Word. A disciple follows a disciplined pattern of living according to the rules and regulations of the One he follows. Discipline is required in order to follow through with God's Kingdom requirements. As believers in Christ Jesus, to live in the blessings of God, a disciplined pattern of behavior is necessary for every aspect of family life. In the financial realm, through reading and understanding God's Word, we can establish this disciplined pattern. For it is God who gives us the power, i.e., the ability to prosper.

In contemporary terms, as it relates to finances, we can use the term budget as this disciplined pattern or a Godly Family Financial Plan (GFFP). As we review the following scriptural passages, we are put in position to develop a GFFP that lines up with the Word of God. This kind of planning authorizes us to experience God's supernatural blessings leading to wealth in all of our family life.

Following is a brief review of scripture that provide direction for financial management for 100% of our family finances. Tithing, as previously mentioned, was first mentioned when Abraham gave a tenth of all he had to Melchezidek, King of Salem. (Genesis 14:20, Hebrews 7:2) Malachi 3:10 is probably the most referred to passage regarding the tithe.

> *Bring ye all the tithes into the storehouse, that there may be meat in mine house, and prove me now herewith, saith the LORD of hosts, if I will not open you the windows of heaven, and pour you out a blessing, that there shall not be room enough to receive it.*

The tithe is used to maintain the physical House of God, the church building.

First fruit offering is also mentioned in scripture. This is a separate gift expected when we are blessed with a new income.

> *The first of the firstfruits of thy land thou shalt bring into the house of the LORD thy God. Thou shalt not seethe a kid in his mother's milk.* (Exodus 23:19)

Often a church will have a building fund drive. Building the House of God or any additions to it, are also separate from the tithe. The people of God are expected to bring what is necessary to build God's House. (I Kings 5, Haggai 1) When Solomon was building the Temple. The people brought so much that Solomon had to ask them to stop giving. This indicates the people of God had something, i.e., wealth, to give.

So, we start our GFFP with the tithe, the first 10% of our 100%. First fruits and building fund monies are added as they occur. Also included in our GFFP are taxes. Jesus admonished the disciples to give to Caesar, the government, what is due the government. Ouch, that one hurts, but it is our obligation as citizens. (Mark 12:14-17)

Also, the following passage implies that that those who preach the Gospel are to be cared for by those to whom they preach. There is no set amount or percentage commanded. Perhaps, in planning a GFFP, it would be wise to set aside funds for those that you receive the teaching/preaching of the Gospel from.

> *Do ye not know that they which minister about holy things live of the things of the temple? and they which wait at the altar are partakers with the altar? Even so hath the Lord ordained that they which preach the gospel should live of the gospel. I Corinthians 9:13-14*

However, many churches give their pastors a salary. Often it is adequate enough to cover their family needs. So, this may not be an area of concern for your family. Let the Holy Spirit guide you. The pastor may at times have a need that can be met through sensitive congregants who are willing to allow God to direct them in the disbursement of the finances that he has entrusted to them.

Another financial concern, probably the area that brings on the most concern, is caring for our families. 1 Timothy 5:8 states, *"But if any provide not for his own, and specially for those of his own house, he hath denied the faith, and is worse than an infidel."* Caring for our families is an important matter to God. A Christian that does not take care of his or her family is considered as an unbeliever in God's estimation.

Another passage admonishes believers to take care of the widows in our families.

> *Honour widows that are widows indeed. But if any*

widow have children or nephews, let them learn first to shew piety at home, and to requite their parents: for that is good and acceptable before God. (1 Timothy 5:3-4)

Matthew 15:4-6 emphasizes the importance that God attaches to His people caring for their parents. Many cultures honor this command, either through family expectation or training. It is important then to set aside some means to help care for parents as appropriate and/or needed.

"For God commanded, saying, 'Honor your father and your mother'; and, 'He who curses father or mother, let him be put to death.' But you say, 'Whoever says to his father or mother, "Whatever profit you might have received from me is a gift to God"— 'then he need not honor his father or mother.' Thus you have made the commandment of God of no effect by your tradition. (NKJ)

The fatherless, widows (including single parents) and the poor are of utmost importance to the Lord. We are to make certain that we make provision for them. (See James 1:27, Galatians 2:10) Isaiah 58: 6-7 expounds upon the heart that God has for those in a various kinds of need.

Is not this the fast that I have chosen? to loose the bands of wickedness, to undo the heavy burdens, and to let the oppressed go free, and that ye break every yoke? Is it not to deal thy bread to the hungry, and that thou bring the poor that are cast out to thy house? when thou seest the naked, that thou cover him; and that thou hide not thyself from thine own flesh?

Another part of the GFFP is the inclusion of pleasure funds.

And also that every man should eat and drink, and

enjoy the good of all his labour, it is the gift of God.
Ecclesiastes 3:13

Saving and investing are matters of good stewardship. It keeps a family in a secure place ready when unexpected expenses arise. It also allows a family to determine whether they can engage in activities not necessarily covered in the GFFP. (Luke 14:28)

> *For the kingdom of heaven is as a man travelling into a far country, who called his own servants, and delivered unto them his goods. And unto one he gave five talents, to another two, and to another one; to every man according to his several ability; and straightway took his journey. Then he that had received the five talents went and traded with the same, and made them other five talents. And likewise he that had received two, he also gained other two.*
> (Matthew 25:14-17)

Following is a summary of what would be included in a GFFP:

GFFP includes: (not necessarily in this order)
10%:   Tithe
90%:   Immediate family (includes housing, utilities, food, clothing, etc.)
Mother & Father
Family Widows
Government/Taxes
Preacher of the Gospel
Outreach to poor, fatherless and widows
Family pleasure
Saving & Investing
100%

After fulfilling the GFFP according the scriptural passages presented, there is nothing left over, like the manna that fell daily for the Israelites in the wilderness. God's faithful provision for them. To the average Christian family, unfortunately, this type of family financial management would cause great sadness, even depression. It looks as though God doesn't give us any room; that he doesn't care for us.

To work hard and have nothing left is disheartening. However, if we apply God's principles, i.e., obey His commands, blessings and wealth follow. The supernatural way of God's Kingdom is initiated and begins to be enacted in our family finances and beyond to all that concerns the family.

As we begin to apply this new understanding with the knowledge of God's love for us and a desire to please him, we will begin to experience supernatural blessings and wealth that keeps a family that follows God's order in a "no lack" mode of living.

When we choose to handle our affairs God's way, putting His plan into action, our family life is enhanced. As we increase, we are able to be a blessing to others. We enter into a cycle of giving and receiving, God's sowing and reaping process (Galatians 6:7)

I acknowledge that this revelation about godly financial management may be God's specific plan for my family and not yours. However, I challenge you to prayerfully read and meditate upon these passages of scripture. Discuss it with your family as appropriate to their ages. Seek the Lord to learn the specific way that he would have your family handle the 100% finances that he entrusts to your care. Whatever He says, put it into action. Your family will be blessed beyond finances.

> *But one who looks intently at the perfect law, the*
> *{law} of liberty, and abides by it, not having become*
> *a forgetful hearer but an effectual doer, this man*
> *shall be blessed in what he does. (James 1:25)*

Note: For a full Bible study and practical application regarding financial management seek out biblically based experts in financial management.

CHAPTER NINE

Review

Name: _____
Class:_____
Period: _____
Date: _____

Read each question carefully, then answer accordingly.

1. Give an explanation of good stewardship.

2. Who is the steward? Who is the owner?

3. Stewardship involves a level of_____ and_____ in the owner.

4. A disciple follows a _____ _____of living according to the rules of the One he follows._

5. Regarding finances, a disciplined pattern can be termed a budget or

_____   _____
_____   _____.

6. Name at least 5 items included in the type of budget discussed:

1)_____ 2)_____

3)_____ 4)_____

5)_____

7. The 10% or tithe is optional and depends on whether or not you trust the preacher. (Circle the correct answer)

True   False

8) Quote one Bible verse or passage mentioned in this chapter:

_____

_____

_____

_____

_____

9) Wealth includes:

a)_____ b))_____

c)_____

10) Obeying God's commands brings _____and wealth.

Fruit for Family Issues

"If you want to make it right, you've got to put up a fight"

G od's goal for mankind is to be fruitful and multiply. This can take place in many ways throughout family life and does not apply to childbearing only. When we bear good fruit, we tend to multiply because others are affected and want the good fruit that they have seen or experienced or are influenced and begin to imitate the good fruit. Just the same, rotten fruit can be multiplied, however will produce many problems and eventual destruction.

Family Life does not come without problems or issues. As issues arise in our families, it is important that we address them in a way that pleases God. Proverbs tells us that when our ways are pleasing to God, even our enemies are at peace with us. (Proverbs 16:7) This means that those that are on our side will either be pleased or at peace with us.

God has given us a picture of how His love is put into action:

> *Love endures long and is patient and kind; love never is envious nor boils over with jealousy; is not boastful or vainglorious, does not display itself haughtily. It is not conceited—arrogant and inflated with pride; it is not rude (unmannerly), and does not*

act unbecomingly. Love [God's love in us] does not insist on its own rights or its own way, for it is not self- seeking; it is not touchy or fretful or resentful; it takes no account of the evil done to it—-pays no attention to a suffered wrong. It does not rejoice at injustice and unrighteousness, but rejoices when right and truth prevail. Love bears up under anything and everything that comes, is ever ready to believe the best of every person, its hopes are fadeless under all circumstances and it endures everything [without weakening]. Love never fails— never fades out or becomes obsolete or comes to an end.

(1 Corinthians 13:4-8, Amplified Bible)

One way of dealing with family issues effectively is by applying Gods' love to our daily way of living. Rather than wait for a problem to arise, family members can be proactive by choosing to live out the different aspects of this passage in relating to one another on a regular basis. Then when a conflict arises, the family is bent toward responding in love.

Galatians 5:22-23 discusses the <u>fruit of the Spirit</u>. This is the fruit that we want to discuss and display when dealing with family issues.

But the fruit of the Spirit is love, joy, peace, long-suffering, gentleness, goodness, faith, Meekness, temperance: against such there is no law. (KJV)

There are <u>nine fruit of the Spirit</u>. These are the fruit of having the Holy Spirit in our lives. Through the indwelling of the Holy Spirit that we received at salvation and the baptism in the Holy Spirit that we receive if we ask God (Ephesians 1:13, Luke 11: 13), we are in a position to exhibit the qualities or characteristics of the Spirit. They are already in us; we must put them into action. It is a choice that we make. As a reminder, the flesh wars after the spirit and the spirit wars after the flesh. However, when we choose to walk in the Spirit, we will not fulfill the lusts of the flesh. (Romans 8:5, Galatians 5: 16-17)

Regarding these fruit of the Spirit, The Amplified version of Galatians 5:22-23 reads:

> *But the fruit of the (Holy) Spirit, [the work that His presence within accomplishes]-is love, joy (gladness), peace, patience (an even temper, forbearance), kindness, goodness (benevolence), faithfulness, (Meekness, humility) gentleness, self-control (self-restraint, contingence). Against such things there is no law [that can bring a charge].*

In the book <u>God in You: Releasing the Power of the Holy Spirit in Your Life</u>, the author, David Jeremiah discusses the fruit of the Holy Spirit and how it operates in the life of the Believer. He suggests that Paul in organizing these characteristics was divinely inspired so that they literally describe every part of who we are in Christ. He notes a three-part breakdown of the fruit of the Spirit.

The first part, he says, describes our personal experience with God; love, joy, and peace. The second part describes our personal relationships with others; patience, kindness, and goodness. The third part describes our personal development as people; faithfulness, gentleness, and self-control. (p.129) These fruit, together, represent Christlikeness.

Let us look at the definition of these nine fruit:

Love (agape)

It is not by coincident that love is noted as the first fruit of the Holy Spirit. As we previously discussed, God is love and love comes from God. (I John 4:7-8) Once receiving Jesus Christ into our hearts the Holy Spirit sheds His love abroad in our hearts. (Romans 5:5) This love cannot compare with human love.

The Greeks have four words that describe love. Eros is the romantic/sexual love. Phileo is friendship love. Storge is affectionate love or some term it, family love. Agape, the love that is given to us by the Spirit, is the unconditional love of God. It is the primary way that God expresses Himself.

This love can only be effectively operated when imparted to us by the Holy Spirit. Humans do not have the ability to exhibit agape apart from God's Spirit. It is a self-giving action for the benefit of others, not necessarily an emotion. The best example of this love is Christ's self-giving on the Cross. (Dictionary of Paul and His Letters, Editors Gerald F. Hawthorne, Ralph P. Martin, and Daniel G. Reid, InterVarsity Press: 1993, p. 318) It is a caring for and seeking the highest good of another person without motive of personal gain. (Full Life Study Bible, p.1819)

An interesting note is that the fruit of God's Spirit correlates with the character description of God's love in I Corinthians 13:4-8.

Galatians 5:22	**I Corinthians 13**
• Joy	- Love *rejoices* in truth (vs.6)
• Peace	- Love thinks no evil, but lives in peace with others (v.5)
• Long-suffering/Patience	- Love suffers long (v.4)
• Kindness	- Love does not behave rudely (v. 5)
• Goodness	- Love does not envy and is not prideful (v. 5)
• Faith/Faithfulness)	- Love believes all things (v.7)
• Meekness/Gentleness	- Love does not seek its own (v. 5)
• Temperance/Self-control	- Love is not provoked, is under control

From: Jeremiah, David, <u>God in You: Releasing the Power of the Holy Spirit in Your Life</u>, Multnomah Publishers, 1998.

Love is first and foremost in our entire lifestyle as a believer in Christ Jesus. It is the trademark that causes others to see that we are disciples of Jesus Christ. (John 13:34-35)

Joy (chara)

The last part of Nehemiah 8:10 says *"... the joy of the Lord is your strength."* This joy is very different than happiness. Happiness, as many explain, depends on what happens. When things are bad than you are sad, when things are good than you are glad. Happiness is an emotion that fluctuates with situations or circumstances of life.

Joy, on the other hand, is a continually abiding presence of the Spirit of God that causes us to have an inner rejoicing even in the midst of trials. It protects us from despair and aids us in our grief. Joy helps us to maintain or regain our spiritual fervor as we combat the troubles that this life on earth brings.

I believe that joy is connected to purity of heart. When our hearts are clean before the Lord, we are able to freely flow in the joy of the Lord. M. Basilea Schlink in her book entitled Repentance - The Joy-Filled Life, says "repentance is a creative, life giving power that brings joy." (p.23) True Christians rejoice in their salvation regardless as to the circumstances of this life. Those who repent of their sins and receive Jesus Christ as Savior and Lord are filled with a joy that this world cannot take away.

They have entered into eternal life with the hope of glory, which is greatly opposed, to the temporal life that once was our only hope. As forgiveness and repentance remains a normal aspect of the life of a Christian, the heart remains pure allowing us to continually experience the joy that was received at salvation.

Peace - (eirene)

Peace is the quietness of heart and mind that is based on the knowledge that all is well between the believer and his or her heavenly Father. (FLSB, p.1819) Spirit-filled believers have true peace no matter what is going on around them. It controls their emotions. It gives them calmness when their human spirit would rush into panic. (Jeremiah, p.116)

God's peace passes our human understanding. (Philippians 4:7) It keeps our hearts and minds through Christ Jesus. It is through the redemptive work on the Cross of Christ that our peace was won. (Isaiah 53:5) Jesus tells us that He left us His peace, which is not the same as the peace this world proclaims.

> *Peace I leave with you, my peace I give unto you:*
> *not as the world giveth, give I unto you. Let not your*
> *heart be troubled, neither let it be afraid.*
>
> *John 14:27 (KJV)*

Peace is the tranquillity ministered to believers to sustain them in life. (Hawthorne, p.318) We are later admonished by Paul the Apostle to let the peace of God rule in our hearts. The Amplified Version of the Bible states *"and let the peace (soul harmony which comes) from the Christ rule (act as umpire continually) in your hearts - deciding and settling with finality all questions that arise in your minds -[in that peaceful state] to which [as members of Christ's] one body, you were called [to live]. And be thankful-appreciative, giving praise to God always.*

The key to this verse is that we are to let God's peace rule. Even though Jesus gave us His peace, it is up to the believer to activate that peace by allowing it to serve as umpire continually in our hearts.

Patience - (Makrothymia)

Patience or long-suffering is a quality that helps us in our relationships with others including God. It requires that we "wait" for the desired thing with a patience that expresses God's love to others. "It is a positive value embracing steadfastness and staying power." (Hawthorne, p. 318) The Greek word that describes this quality of the Holy Spirit is *macrothumia.* It means, "long temper." A person with a long temper stays in control of his feelings when dealing with other people. (Jeremiah, p.117)

It includes being slow to speak and slow to anger. When a person exhibits patience, also termed patient endurance, they are making known to others where their trust lies. In most situations requiring patience, the only way to operate in the patience that comes from the Spirit is through the inner knowing that God is in control (I Chronicles 29:11,12). That is, believing in the heart that *all things* are under God's realizing that He works all things together for the good of those who love Him and are called according to His purpose. (Romans 8:28)

Therefore our acts of spirit-led patience are genuine and not just a "waiting" because we have no other choice.

Kindness - (Chrestotes)

Kindness is being nice to others out of a genuine and caring heart for them and is without selfish motive. "Kindness is a quality of God's gracious attitude and actions towards sinners (Romans 2:4, Ephesians 2:7, Titus 3: 4)." (Hawthorne, p.318) It actually is God's love in action through the believer. It is something given to another regardless as to their actions or attitudes. Kindness is moral excellence in character or demeanor. (Strongs #5544) Kindness is behavior with a positive attitude attached to it. When a person engages in an act of kindness, others notice that person's genuineness and can almost feel the genuineness of their heart.

Goodness - (Agathosyne)

Goodness is a zeal for truth and righteousness and a hatred of evil; it can be expressed through acts of kindness or in rebuking or correcting evil. (FLSB, p.1819)

A good person is one in who most people trust. Their actions or attitudes in a given situation are predictable because of the good naturedness that others can see and sense about them.

This quality is expressed through the way that we handle conflicting situations or situations of compromise. Goodness will show itself by standing for what is right or true regardless of the impact that it might have on self and at times, others. Rather than compromise, or attempt to please others, this quality expresses itself by engaging in the behavior, attitude, or conversation that leads to the godly standard.

Faithfulness - (Pistis)

Faithfulness is expressed through integrity and loyalty. It is a firm and unswerving loyalty to a person whom one is united by promise, commitment, trustworthiness, and honesty. (FLSB, p.1819) A person filled with the Spirit of God is steadfast and unswerving in his convictions, which become who He is in Christ Jesus.

Proverbs 20:6 says, *"Who can find a faithful man?"* The faithful man is known by what others see and say about him rather than by what he says about himself. This is an action quality. It is acted out by the way a person goes about his daily living and how he incorporates his belief in Christ Jesus into all that he does and says. Faithfulness in a person means that they are dependable. They carry out the commitments that they have received of God. They can be trusted with confidences and responsibilities because their convictions are in Jesus Christ, His ways and His Word and their commitment is ultimately to Him.

Gentleness - (Prautes)

Gentleness or meekness is the humility of Jesus Christ operating through the believer. Note Philippians 2:5-8

> *Let this mind be in you, which was also in Christ Jesus:*
> *Who, being in the form of God, thought it not robbery to be equal with God:*
> *But made himself of no reputation, and took upon him the form of a servant, and was made in the likeness of men: And being found in fashion as a man, he humbled himself, and became obedient unto death, even the death of the cross.* (KJV)

Gentleness/meekness is an inner strength that pervades the believer's being as he or she chooses to yield to it. It is a submissive quality that is quiet and lowly. Often it is perceived as weakness or foolishness in its inaction to criticisms or wrongs done by others. It is a quiet confidence that does not allow shame or disheartedness to have the final say and does not give up on believing in God's grace and goodness.

> *For the which cause I also suffer these things: nevertheless I am not ashamed: for I know whom I have believed, and am persuaded that he is able to keep that which I have committed unto him against that*

day. 2 Timothy 1:12 (KJV)

It is a power that is under control. Through testings and challenges of life, a person who exhibits gentleness is often steady in personality and attitude. They are usually seen rather than heard. Others recognize their meek and quiet spirit and either admire it or resent it.

Self-control - (Enkrateia)
Self-control is mastering one's own desires and passions, including remaining faithful in relationships and to commitments as ordained by God. (FLSB, p.1819) Paul talks about being disciplined and its necessity in preaching the Gospel of Jesus Christ.

> *Know ye not that they which run in a race run all,*
> *but one receiveth the prize? So run, that ye may*
> *obtain. And every man that striveth for the mastery*
> *is temperate in all things. Now they do it to obtain a*
> *corruptible crown; but we an incorruptible.*
> *I therefore so run, not as uncertainly; so fight I, not*
> *as one that beateth the air:*
> *But I keep under my body, and bring it into subjec-*
> *tion: lest that by any means, when I have preached*
> *to others, I myself should be a castaway.*
> *1 Corinthians 9:24-27 (KJV)*

The other word used for self-control is temperance. It speaks of a decision to abstain from an attitude, behavior, thought, people, place or thing, for the sake of holiness. It is motivated by a human spirit that has been indwelled by the Holy Spirit and has a desire to please God. The fruit came through and operates by the Holy Spirit. God's Spirit is holy. Its very nature is holiness. There tends to be an emphasis on the "Spirit" and not on "Holy." The fruit of God's Spirit are intended to further emphasize the holiness of God.

George Verwer, in his writing, The Revolution of Love, says that the fruit of the Spirit cannot come apart from holiness. Therefore, self-control or temperance operates out of an aim toward holiness. Its goal is to touch no unholy thing. The believer is given this spiritual quality as an aid to help in abstaining from those situations, people, attitudes, or behaviors and things that would corrupt its nature.

This fruit that is desperately needed to help us to walk in the Spirit so we do not fulfill the lusts of the flesh, is probably the one least activated by the contemporary Christian. Rather than self-control or temperance, we see a rise in compulsive, lustful and addictive behaviors amongst believers in Jesus Christ. Paul discusses the struggle to avoiding lusts and following after righteousness in Romans chapter seven.

> *Wherefore the law is holy, and the commandment holy, and just, and good.*
> *Was then that which is good made death unto me? God forbid. But sin, that it might appear sin, working death in me by that which is good; that sin by the commandment might become exceeding sinful.*
> *For we know that the law is spiritual: but I am carnal, sold under sin.*
> *For that which I do I allow not: for what I would, that do I not; but what I hate, that do I. If then I do that which I would not, I consent unto the law that it is good. Now then, it is no more I that do it, but sin that dwelleth in me. For I know that in me (that is, in my flesh,) dwelleth no good thing: for to will is present with me; but how to perform that which is good I find not. For the good that I would I do not: but the evil which I would not, that I do. Now if I do that I would not, it is no more I that do it, but sin that dwelleth in me. I find then a law, that, when I would do good, evil is present with me. For I delight in the law of God after the inward man: But I see another law in my members, warring against the law of my mind, and bringing me into captivity to the law of sin which is in my members. O wretched man that I am! who shall deliver me from the body of this death? I thank God through Jesus Christ our Lord. So then*

with the mind I myself serve the law of God; but with
the flesh the law of sin. vs. 12-21 (KJV)

He admits his struggle acknowledging how difficult it is to overcome the lusts that dwell in his flesh. However, he makes it clear that these things can be overcome through Jesus Christ our Lord. As the believer yields himself to the Word of God and the Holy Spirit (the Spirit and the Word agree), the fruit of self-control/temperance becomes stronger giving the believer greater ability to abstain from those things that are destructive to a holy lifestyle.

Lastly, this quality of the Spirit, more so than the others require a daily dying to self in order to operate effectively. Water baptism and baptism of the Holy Spirit are often the key to breaking the barriers to exhibiting the fruit of self-control.

Now that we have a thorough understanding of the character qualities that we have received through God's Spirit, it is important to make the decision to operate in them. The reminder here is that the option is to be a carnal Christian or a Spirit led Christian. It is left up to you and your family. It requires a personal decision with an action of confirmation. Once we begin and continue to put the fruit into action, the supernatural power of God empowers and enables us to continue to live by the Spirit with lesser difficulty than at first.

CHAPTER TEN

Review

Name: _____

Class:_____

Period: _____

Date: _____

Read each question carefully, then print the letter of the correct answer on the line next to the question.

1. Name the fruit of the Holy Spirit. _____

    _____

    _____

2. Give a definition or description of two fruit. _____

    _____

    _____

3. I Corinthians 13:4-8 discusses God's _____.

4. The flesh is _____

5. God's desire in the beginning was that man be _____

    and _____

6. Two Scriptural passages are said to correlate with one another regarding God's love. Name them. _____

    _____

7. Knowing the fruit of the Holy Spirit is important, but _____ is more important.

8. The difference between the Holy Spirit and any other spirit is that it is_____

9. Why is it of no coincidence that love is the first fruit mentioned?

   _____

   _____

10. When the fruit of the Spirit are in operation, who are we most like?_____

    _____

CHAPTER ELEVEN

Moving From Ungodly to Godly

*"Godliness yields fruit of righteousness for this life
and the life to come"*

As we discussed in the previous chapter, God through Jesus Christ and by His (Holy) Spirit has given us fruit that signify that we are in relationship with Him; that we are like Him. These character qualities are given to us at salvation, however it is up to us to operate them. (Philippians 2:12)

In order for your family life to be what God desires, the family members must make the choice to incorporate the fruit of the Holy Spirit into their relationships, circumstances and situations on a daily basis. As the family chooses God's way of doing things (righteousness), they are empowered by the Holy Spirit to override their flesh to a greater and greater degree.

This, however, is a process of choices. Remember the first fruit mentioned is the fruit of love. Also, we learned that God is love. Love than is the "spirit" in which God operates. Everything that God did or has done or has planned for us is an act of His love. *For God so loved the world that He sent His only begotten Son... For God sent not his Son into the world to condemn the world; but that the world through him might be saved. (John 3:16-17)*

As children of God made in His image and likeness and as disciples of Jesus Christ, our mandate as Christians is to exhibit these fruit.

> *Abide in me, and I in you. As the branch cannot bear fruit of itself, except it abide in the vine; no more can ye, except ye abide in me. I am the vine, ye are the branches: He that abideth in me, and I in him, the same bringeth forth much fruit: for without me ye can do nothing. If a man abide not in me, he is cast forth as a branch, and is withered; and men gather them, and cast them into the fire, and they are burned. If ye abide in me, and my words abide in you, ye shall ask what ye will, and it shall be done unto you. Herein is my Father glorified, that ye bear much fruit; so shall ye be my disciples. John 15:4-8 (KJV)*

The key to *bearing fruit* is that we abide in Christ. That means that we live with a purpose to know Him and be known by Him. Without Him our acts that replicate the fruit of the Holy Spirit are in vain, they have no power. They may bring positive results but will not have lasting resolution to family issues because the family members are operating in their own strength rather than through Christ Jesus. (Philippians 4:13)

Andrew Murray in the Christian classic <u>Abide in Christ</u> discusses the matter of abiding as a *day by day and at this moment activity*. In order to bear fruit, we must pursue Christ daily and moment-by-moment. Our goal as Christians is to remain in Him at all times. Some have made the statement, "let me lay my religion down for a minute." What they mean is, "let me operate in the flesh to handle this matter that perturbed me, then I'll go back to operating in the Spirit."

This kind of attitude and behavior does not please God and does not bring godly resolution to the matter at hand. Although some of the issues that we face in our family relationships are tough and make it somewhat difficult to ignore the desire to operate in the flesh, God has given us the ability to walk by the Spirit. And it can be done! (Romans 8:14)

Spending time in the Word of God (personal time and time hearing the preached Word and in a Bible study), prayer, praise and worship (personal and in the fellowship with other saints) helps to keep us in an abiding posture. It also helps us to grow in our knowledge of the Lord and in developing our relationship with Him.

Let's review the fruit of the Holy Spirit: *Love * joy * peace *patience   *kindness   *gentleness   *meekness   *self-control.* Understanding each fruit, and having a heart that seeks after God, empowers the family to apply these fruit to their family life. Following are practical issues that arise in family relationships and life itself. Next to each one is a fruit of the Spirit that most aptly corresponds as a way of handling the issues presented.

Family Issue	**Fruit of the Spirit**
• Someone who has repeatedly talked negatively about you to others is now in trouble and needs your help	- **Love and Meekness**
• You just learned that your loved one is terminally ill	- **Peace**
• You've had multiple deaths in your family and now you are faced with another family crisis	- **Joy**
• Your family member has made a decision that to you is foolish and ridiculous and hurts your feelings. You are angry with them.	- **Kindness**
• You are told by a co-worker that you can have an item that belongs to the company	- **Goodness**

- Instead of obeying your instructions
  not to throw the ball in the house, your
  child does so and breaks your favorite
  piece of crystal   **- Gentleness/
  Meekness**

- You love pork rolls, however the doctor
  has ordered that you discontinue eating
  pork   **- Temperance/
  Self- control**

- You are having problems in your
  marriage that have stressed you out and
  you want to end it   **- Faithfulness**

- The family financial situation is in
  a terrible state. You have learned about
  giving and have been tithing and giving
  offerings. Prosperity has not come.   **- Patience/
  Longsuffering**

Think about your own family and some issues that you have had to deal with. Have you responded to them in the spirit or in the flesh? Can you see how you can apply the fruit of the Spirit to that issue? As hard as it might be to put down the flesh, once applying the fruit of the Spirit, God will be pleased and eventually you will notice a change taking place; in you or in others towards you.

In Chapters Seven and Eight we discussed enhancers to family life. Applying these along with the fruit of the Spirit to your family life allows God's Spirit of love to flow in your home. This will cause the family to develop intimacy and care more for one another. As the family draws closer to God and to one another, caring behaviors begin to manifest.

"Caring behaviors are the lifeblood of a relationship. They are those small, frequent acts of sensitivity, kindness and caring that let our loved ones know they are important to us. They are signs that we matter and that our relationship is important." (<u>PEERS: Skills</u>

for Emotional Intimacy, PAIRS Foundation, Ltd., 1999)

The more that we study and learn God's Word and the greater reverence that we have towards Him, the more that we will willingly apply His way of doing things to our personal and family life. The godlier we become. As time passes, you and others begin to recognize a change in you and/or your relationships. However, as you grow in your walk with God you will at times have to repent for an ungodly action or attitude.

It is necessary to apply patience to yourself and others in your growth. Growth is a process. Sanctification is an ongoing process that does not end until we are face to face with the Lord. To get upset because of imperfections is a fleshly expectation and response. God looks on the heart. *When we mess up, we fess up,* quickly. This is what pleases the Lord. Ask for other's and the Lord's forgiveness when you respond in an ungodly manner. Forgive yourself and move on. Apply forgiveness when someone else sins against you. Then, move on in godliness.

Godly behavior reflects God and is characteristic of a person or family that is devoted to him. Ungodly behavior is opposed to God, does not please Him and reflects the enemy of God, Satan. (John 8:42-44) In order to move from an ungodly family life to a godly family life, it is of utmost importance that the family makes Jesus Christ Savior and Lord of their individual lives. This new life that they receive will flow into the life of the family causing a transformation from ungodly to godly as family members and as the family as a whole put their trust in Him. (Romans 12:1-2)

God states in Deuteronomy 30:19-20:

> *I call heaven and earth to record this day against you, that I have set before you life and death, blessing and cursing: therefore <u>choose life</u>, that both thou and thy seed may live: That thou mayest love the LORD thy God, and that thou mayest obey his voice, and that thou mayest cleave unto him: for he is thy life, and the length of thy days: that thou mayest dwell in the land which the LORD sware unto thy fathers, to Abraham, to Isaac, and to Jacob, to give them.*

Choosing life means choosing to live godly, i.e., being like God. When parents choose life exhibiting, godliness in the whole of their lives, their children are directly affected. Just the same, if parents live ungodly lives, their children are directly affected and are on a path called death. (Of course, however, children can apart from their parents, make a decision for God and change their spiritual course.)

The family that chooses to live godly is set apart by God and has the promise of life (the abundant life and eternal life) operating within their family life. (Psalm 4:3, I Timothy 4:8) They are no longer giving place to the devil because their whole aim and lifestyle is that of pleasing God thus bringing Him glory.

"The light of the righteous shines brightly..."
Proverbs 13:9a

Note: See Appendix VII for a comparison of godly versus ungodly behavioral traits

CHAPTER ELEVEN

Review

Name: _____

Class:_____

Period: _____

Date: _____

In 2 to 5 paragraphs write specific areas and ways in which your family has or plans to move from ungodly family living to the godly living that God desires for you. Use an additional page, if necessary.

CHAPTER TWELVE

Getting It Back

"It's what you do that proves your faith"

Consequences come because of disobeying God's way of doing things, whether intentionally or ignorantly done. These consequences affect family life causing minor issues to major life-debilitating issues. Out of wedlock births, divorce, a breakdown within a family or break-up of a live in situation brings about consequences that our society has accepted as the norm.

Some of these consequences continue for years after the ungodly incident took place and affect many more than the few people involved. A very real example is the dysfunction of children of these family divisions mentioned. Many of you can probably remember a person whom after becoming an adult was still suffering with some form of mental anguish because of the break-up of their family, which took place when they were children. They now have their own family or children that are suffering from lack of proper nurturing and/or the parent's inability to properly provide for them.

Drug addiction, adultery, fornication, abusive relationships, multiple children out of wedlock, absentee fathers (living in or out of the house), overwhelmed mothers, gangs, sexually transmitted diseases, a national triple increase in depression and criminal behaviors are some of the consequences that carry on into the next generation. Although these problems must be addressed in ways specific to the nature of the problem, the root problem must also be addressed.

The root problem is disobedience. As was mentioned in our discussion about breaking generational curses, "the buck has to stop somewhere." The family or a family member can begin the ceasing of the cycle of family sin and destruction by acknowledging the sin (even if ignorantly engaged in), repenting of it for self or on the behalf of the family, forgiving ancestors for bringing judgment upon the family, renouncing the specific sins, and making a confession to engage in righteousness.

Of course, acts that are in line with repentance seal the heartfelt and humble prayer of one whom would choose this route. Behavior, attitudes, and/or speech must begin to change. This is a conscious choice by the individual and/or family. Long-suffering with self and others is necessary because this is not an overnight process. However, it is not one that will take as many years as it did to become a family norm. Choosing to obey God will bring blessings, deliverance, and healing to the individual and family. (See I Samuel 15:22 for discussion)

How does a family begin to put God's plan into action after ignorantly having lived a life opposed to God? It is best to begin to incorporate your new understanding of God's way and Word gently but with resoluteness. I recall when I was introduced to living by the Word. After spending most of my life in and out of the church, I had never clearly understood "how" to live as a Christian. The Bible was not my book for life and living. It was what the preacher used on Sunday and a book that we on rare occasions read.

With this new information and a rededicated heart to God, I became a fanatic. Immediately, I stopped as much of my former lifestyle that I was able to. My music changed, my partying changed, some friendships were changed, where I hung out changed, my perspective changed. At the time I was a single parent and so called independent and carefree, moving up the corporate ladder.

My ambitions changed. The change that was most dramatic and traumatic was my family life. My children were young and accustomed to living good lives, but not godly lives. There is a difference.

When godliness became the pursuit of our home, my children, in a sense, experienced trauma. I did not have the wisdom to know that they needed grace and gentleness in this change. Rather than allowing them to witness my changed life, I expected from them a changed life.

We had wonderful times of fellowship with each other and with other believers. We spent time learning the Word of God together. Our family life had changed and that, because of God's amazing grace. As I reflect on how our lives changed, I share a word of caution. Children have no choice but to follow their parents. Often when parents see the "Light" and begin to change, they are embarrassed when their children exhibit ungodly behaviors. This often causes them to force the children into Christian behavior by punishment if not adhered to.

The children may follow suit. They may enjoy the children's or youth program. They may respond to the discipline for ungodly behavior. It is very important that as parents to be sensitive to the needs of each child and help them to come to the "Light" as you did rather than dragging them to the Light. Set godly standards and explain them to your children. Be careful though, that you do not become legalistic. This can impact your children negatively causing them to deny your faith even when acting out the rules of the faith.

As for spouses, one becoming saved and the other unsaved. Love is always the proper response. Do not let fear take hold of you. Fear and faith in God cannot operate at the same time. Fear that your spouse will not be saved can cause nagging and manipulation as a means to getting them to church or to Christ. Anger because they don't see what you see and continue to live a way you refuse to live may cause you to think that you made a mistake in marrying this spouse or that you have nothing in common to maintain the relationship.

Love suffers long and is patient and kind; God's love. Pray privately for your spouse and children's salvation. Read your Bible but not as a show that you are changed. Let your Bible work through how you relate to your spouse and children. Let love and faithfulness be your fruit. Don't give up. Trust God. The Bible says that godliness with contentment is great gain. (I Timothy 6:6)

Other ways that you can begin to put God's plan into action follows:

- Develop a family mission statement with goals and put it into action
- As a proactive measure, look at ways to incorporate God's love and the fruit of the Holy Spirit to specific issues that your family is challenged by
- Personally, begin to yield to the biblical role that God has ordained for you
- Teach and model for your children character traits that exemplify godliness
- Read through the Bible with an aim to understand God's love and promises to you and your family
- Implement a family financial stewardship plan with all members involved
- Spend time in prayer for your family asking God to show you His purpose/call for each family member and write it down - use as a tool of encouragement
- Work on a particular family enhancer to help your family life become more fruitful
- Respond to past ungodly patterns of behavior with repentance (completely turning from it) or to hurts or sins against you with forgiveness; name them (see appendix II)
- If necessary, enlist the aid of a pastoral or Christian counselor to help steer you and your family in the right direction
- Attend seminars, read books, listen to teaching tapes or watch videos that can help you and/or your family deal with issues specific to your family members
- Incorporate family prayer and intercession into your family life ("a family that prays together, stays together")

Once you have been introduced to biblical mandates, you are no longer in ignorance. Your responsibility is to respond. The response that pleases God is obedience to His Word. This is His will concerning you and your family. When you do not know what to do in a particular situation or how to carry out God's Word, pray. He says in James 1:5, that if anyone lacks wisdom ask Him and He will give it liberally.

He may provide the answer through a message you hear, through a conversation, something you read or any other avenue He chooses. When God speaks, you will have an inward witness that this is God's way and a peace alongside. You may have some apprehension because it is something new; however, God's wisdom brings certain qualities that help us to know whether God's wisdom or man's wisdom is at work.

> *But if ye have bitter envying and strife in your hearts, glory not, and lie not against the truth.*
> *This wisdom descendeth not from above, but is earthly, sensual, devilish. For where envying and strife is, there is confusion and every evil work. But the wisdom that is from above is first pure, then peaceable, gentle, and easy to be intreated, full of mercy and good fruits, without partiality, and without hypocrisy. And the fruit of righteousness is sown in peace of them that make peace.*
> *James 3:14-18*

The sooner that your family puts God's way into action, the sooner that you will experience your family life bearing good fruit and no longer trapped by ignorance and the cycle of sin.

GETTING IT BACK

Scriptural Overview

The gist of this section is to provide some specific and applicable biblical passages to emphasize the importance of choosing and accepting God's way into your family life. Then, taking the necessary steps that will set your family on a "path of righteousness" (continually putting His plan into action). Righteous living brings about sure rewards (Proverbs 11:18) and the fruit will be peace (Isaiah 32:17). This is a promise from God and He does not lie. (Numbers 23:19, Titus 1:2, Hebrews 6:18)

1) When we do not put God's plan into action, in our personal, family and business lives, consequences follow. Below are some consequences:

Consequences

- Dysfunctional, disconnected, unhealthy, ungodly relationships
- Financial problems
- Out of wedlock births
- Family breakdown
- Break-ups, separation, divorce
- Problems with children
- Mental anguish of family members
- Sexual sins
- Drug and other addictions
- Lack of commitment
- Lack of trust in relationships
- Absentee fathers
- Disgruntled or disengaged mothers
- Generational curses leading to self sins
- Role Confusion
- Others

2) Root of Consequences: Disobedience

Deuteronomy 8:19

If you ever forget the LORD your God and follow <u>other gods</u> and worship and bow down to them, I testify against you today that you will surely be destroyed. (NIV)

Deuteronomy 28:15

However, if you do not obey the LORD your God and do not carefully follow all his commands and decrees I am giving you today, <u>all these curses will come upon you and overtake you</u>: You will be cursed in the city and cursed in the country. (NIV)

Romans 1:18-32

The <u>wrath of God is being revealed from heaven</u> against all the godlessness and wickedness of men who suppress the truth by their wickedness, <u>since what may be known about God is plain to them, because God has made it plain to them.</u> For since the creation of the world God's invisible qualities— his eternal power and divine nature— have been clearly seen, being understood from what has been made, so that men are without excuse. For although they knew God, they neither glorified him as God nor gave thanks to him, but their thinking became futile and their foolish hearts were darkened. Although they claimed to be wise, they became fools and exchanged the glory of the immortal God for images made to look like mortal man and birds and animals and reptiles. Therefore God gave them over in the sinful desires of their hearts to sexual impurity for the degrading of their bodies with one another. They exchanged the truth of God for a lie, and worshipped and served created things rather than the Creator— who is forever praised. Amen. Because of this, God gave them over to shameful lusts. Even their women exchanged natural relations for unnatural ones. In the same way the men also abandoned natural relations with women and were inflamed with lust for one another. Men committed indecent acts with other men, and received in themselves the due penalty for their perversion. Furthermore, since *they did not think it worthwhile to retain the knowledge of God, he gave them over to a depraved mind, to do what ought not to be done. They have become filled with every kind of wickedness, evil, greed and depravity. They are full of envy, murder, strife, deceit and malice. They are gossips, slanderers, God-haters, insolent, arrogant and boastful; they invent ways of doing evil; they disobey their parents; they are senseless, faithless, heartless, ruthless. Although they know God's righteous decree that those who do such things deserve death, they not only continue to do these very things but also approve of those who practice them. (NIV)*

2 Timothy 3:1-5

But mark this: <u>There will be terrible times in the last days</u>. People will be lovers of themselves, lovers of money, boastful, proud, abusive, disobedient to their parents, ungrateful, unholy, without love, unforgiving, slanderous, without self-control, brutal, not lovers of the good, treacherous, rash, conceited, lovers of pleasure rather than lovers of God— having a form of godliness but denying its power. Have nothing to do with them. (NIV)

3) Requirements to Reversing the Curse: Choices

- Repentance/Forgiveness (see Appendix II)
- Increase in devotion to God (Mark 12: 29,30 and Matthew 6:33)
- Implement Love & The Fruit of the Spirit
- Consistently put God's ways into action - practically & specifically

Romans 1:5, 6

Through him and for his name's sake, we received grace and apostleship to call people from among all the Gentiles <u>to the obedience that comes from faith</u>. And you also are among those who are called to belong to Jesus Christ. (NIV)

2 Timothy 3:14,15

But as for you, <u>continue in what you have learned and have become convinced of,</u> because you know those from whom you learned it, and how from infancy you have known the holy Scriptures, which are able to make you wise for salvation through faith in Christ Jesus. (NIV)

Philippians 3:12-16

Not that I have already obtained all this, or have already been made perfect, but I press on to take hold of that for which Christ Jesus took hold of me. Brothers, I do not consider myself yet to have taken hold of it. But one thing I do: Forgetting what is behind and straining toward what is ahead, I press on toward the goal to win the prize for which God has called me heavenward in Christ Jesus. All of us who are mature should take such a view of things. And if on some point you think differently, that too God will make clear to you. <u>Only let us live up to what we have already attained.</u> (NIV)

CHAPTER TWELVE

Review

Name: _____

Class:_____

Period: _____

Date: _____

Final Assignment

Choose One topic, then complete in writing or through an in class-room presentation.

- Develop a family mission statement with goals and put it into action

- As a proactive measure, look at ways to incorporate God's love and the fruit of the Holy Spirit to specific issues that your family is challenged by

- Personally, begin to yield to the biblical role that God has ordained for you

- Teach and model for your children character traits that exemplify godliness

- Read through the Bible with an aim to understand God's love and promises to you and your family

- Spend time in prayer for your family asking God to show you His purpose/call for each family member and write it down - use as a tool of encouragement

- Work on a particular family enhancer to help your family life become more fruitful

- Respond to past ungodly patterns of behavior with repentance (working on completely turning from that behavior) or to hurts or sins against you with forgiveness; name them (see Appendix II)

- If necessary, enlist the aid of a pastoral or Christian counselor to help steer your family in the right direction

- Attend a seminar, read a book, listen to teaching tapes or watch videos that can help you and/or your family deal with issues specific to your family members

- Incorporate family prayer and intercession into your family life ("a family that prays together, stays together")

Author's Testimony

Family life submitted to God and His ways has been a passion of mine for many years. Because of my personal experience of a life of living in and experiencing the affects of the sin cycle, my goal is to help others get out of the death trap. In no way am I saying that I have arrived or that my family and I are perfect. We are far from it. However, many of us have made a decision that has caused "the working things together for good" process to begin in our lives. (Romans 8:28)

That decision was not left at accepting Jesus Christ as Savior. We made (and are still making) the decision to make Jesus Lord over our lives. Our aim is to allow God to discipline us, to cleanse us of unrighteousness, to prune and purge us of ungodliness, to correct us in our wrongs, to heal us of deep-seated hurts, and to deliver us from demonic bondage. This is not always an easy process. The process itself is sometimes painful. But it is a temporary process and the gain is far worth it.

Even in the process of God working in us to will and to do of His good pleasure, in His grace and mercy, He uses us to bless others with our testimony of His faithfulness in where we are thus far. We work at not taking His grace and mercy for granted. We realize that our situations could be worse and that many of us could be living in mental institutions or dead. But we are not. As Bishop T. D. Jakes, so eloquently says, *"we are still here!"*

We are here now with purpose. Purpose to pursue God and His plans for our family life. One area that God's blessings have been manifested is in the lives of my grandchildren. Sexual sins, broken relationships within the family, divorce, parents ignorant as to the proper care of children, these and others are some of the consequences that our family, for years, probably generations have experienced.

God has blessed me with seven grandchildren whom before coming into this world heard about Jesus Christ and experienced His peace while still in the womb. My daughter and her husband are committed Christians whom are seeking the purposes of God for their family. They are committed to imparting godliness into their children with a goal to prepare them for the purposes and destiny of God for their lives. This for my family, is breakthrough.

The difference in these children is evident. I know that they are not perfect and realize that life challenges everyone and that we may have to deal with some hard issues as they develop. However, I know that they are not subject to the spiritual bondage and sin cycle that generations before us were subject to. God is still at work and we are continuing to choose life rather the death.

This is my hope for you and your family. That you make the choices that lead to life and refuse those ways that keep you in a death trap. Even when that choice is a difficult one, remember that you will bear fruit of righteousness when you choose God. And obedience brings blessings even if you do have to wait for them.

Family life is the institution that God instituted and ordained. He wants us to experience His Love and Life even through the storms of this temporal passage. Don't pursue perfection, pursue God. He will do the work in and through your family that will keep you in a place of humility and worship. You, then, will grow in your reverence for Him and increase in your love for Him. Faithful is He who called you and He will do it! (I Thessalonians 5:24) God is faithful to help His children live lives of godliness and holiness as His children willingly choose to follow after Him. Remember, God will help you put His plan into action on a daily basis, if you ask Him. Just commit to do what you can do to *get it back!*

Please pray this prayer with me:

Dear God,

Thank you for your love. Thank you for making a way for my family and me. Forgive us of our past sins and sin cycle. Deliver us from evil. Show us the ways to change our lives to ways that please you. You are the Potter, we are your clay. Make us and mold us to live according to your way. Give us your wisdom, help us to live lives of love. We let go of the old and accept the new that is in You. I proclaim that my family life is the salt, light and a testimony of your Presence that will affect other families. Thank you Lord for your awesome grace and mercy. It is a new season for my family. We choose you. In Jesus' Name. AMEN

If you have not entered into a relationship with God through Jesus Christ, read these verses and follow them:

> *"That if you confess with your mouth, "Jesus is Lord," and believe in your heart that God raised him from the dead, you will be saved. For it is with your heart that you believe and are justified, and it is with your mouth that you confess and are saved."* (NIV)
> Romans 10: 9,10

If you have slipped in your relationship with God and want to return to Him, read the following verse and follow it:

> *"Again and again I sent all my servants the prophets to you. They said, "Each of you must turn from your wicked ways and reform your actions; do not follow other gods to serve them. Then you will live in the land I have given to you and your fathers..."* (NIV)
> Jeremiah 35:15

> *"Let us search and try our ways, and turn again to the LORD. Let us lift up our heart with our hands*

unto God in the heavens."

Lamentations 3:40-41

Honestly repent of your sins (of doing things your way or the way of the world) and ask (allow) Jesus to take charge of your life. Locate a church in your area that is centered on Jesus Christ as Savior and Lord that teaches the whole Bible, and has opportunity for relationship development with other Christians and/or provides classes that help you in your spiritual growth and development.

Last Words

In the early 90's, I wrote a thesis paper in which I proposed biblically based family seminars geared to the African American urban culture. Now ten plus years later, as I reviewed it to extract from it so as to expound upon the subject of the African American family, I was saddened to acknowledge that the situation in the African American community (such as is in America as a whole), has gotten worse.

African American churches as well as interracial and intergenerational churches are on the rise, in number and in scope of influence. Yet, the crisis in the African American community is also on the rise. Something is grossly wrong. It would appear that as the church grows, the crisis situations would decrease. Something is amiss.

It is time for the church of the True and Living God to take a stand! It is time for the people, who are the Church, to decide to live like God and not just for His benefits. We are losing a generation to ungodliness and have lost many in generations gone by. We have lost them through ignorance. Lack of biblical knowledge and understanding was the problem in earlier years.

However, there is no lack of knowledge in the Twenty First Century. Books, tapes, movies, CD's, DVD's in cars, computers on cell phones, Christian TV and many other technological advances makes knowledge easily assessable. Understanding, however, is still a problem. Proverbs 4:7 declares: *"In all thy getting, get understanding."* Understanding leads the way to application. Application is the essence of wisdom.

With the increase in church attendance and in outreaches to African American communities, understanding and application are still missing. I propose two possibilities of missing ingredients. One, relationship development and, two, true models of godly living. God made His people for relationship. That is, relationship with Him and with others. Truly knowing God and His ways comes through a growing relationship with Him. Knowledge of God is good, but unapplied knowledge amounts to nothing.

Relationship with God empowers us to relate to others. Others may be different than you are. They may not live where you live or talk the way you talk. Through the love that God pours into the hearts of Christians, relating to others different than you are becomes easier. The church, the people who make up the church, must begin to live a life outside of the church that is worthy of the calling Christian. (Ephesians 4:1)

To see true and lasting change in African American communities, and in America as a whole, the people who know God and live according to His order must live that Life in the open for others to see. It is crucial, urgent, and a matter of life versus death for many African Americans.

Building relationships outside of the church, with people who may not ever attend your church, brings the church to them in a way that will impact their lives and reach them for Christ much more than a one time Sunday morning experience. This is not to discount the power of God that flows during a first time visit to a church. The emphasis is in the relationship of one who is "the church" with one who may be ignorant of the true operation of "the church," the body of Christ.

Out of these types of relationships, trust and accountability are developed. Modeling appropriate behavior and conversation are informally taught. Inquiries about the Scripture or godliness in general can be made without embarrassment while families know whom they can go to when in conflict. Classes can be established right in the community to teach biblical principles, one or two families at a time. As they learn, implement the principles and begin to change, they will be used to affect others. And the beat goes on.

This is the Biblical model for life and living. Its' application has far reaching effects, effects beyond the African American community and will spill over into the life of all Americans as we live lives of godliness at work, at play, at home. We, the church, must change to experience change. We must grow to experience growth. We must accept God's way of living to have a nation that chooses to live God's way. We, the people of God, can do it! We must do it! We have the power. It lies within us; *"...greater is He that is in you than he that is in the world." (I John 4:4)*

For the sake of our children and children's children, for the sake of the Kingdom of God on earth, we must take a genuine stand. We must regain our focus for living this life we call Christianity. We must do what Jesus said we would do.

> *"Most assuredly, I say to you, he who believes in Me, the works that I do he will do also; and greater works than these he will do, because I go to My Father. John 14:12 (NKJ)*

This book, dear reader, has been written to provoke you to action. It is written to encourage you to make the necessary changes in your family life. Perhaps, to affect you so dramatically that you affect change in others. Let yourself be open to God and a life changing lifestyle as you implement godliness through biblical principles in your own life modeling such for those you influence. *You are the light of the world!* My prayers are with you, but more than that, Jesus is making intercession for your family's success!

ANSWER SHEETS

Chapter Five

Answer Sheet

Name: _____

Class: _____

Period: _____

Date: _____

_____

Read each question carefully, then write (T) for true and (F) for false on the line next to the question.

1. __F__ Without fully knowing God a family is completely destroyed.

2. __T__ A plan is a premeditated intentional purpose.

3. __F__ The word "family" has one Greek definition.

4. __T__ God was in relationship from the beginning.

5. __F__ Covenant relationship with God is an option that we can choose when we become Christians.

6. __T__ Scripture clearly states that God is love.

7. __T__ Male plus female equals man.

8. __F__ God's plan for family life is automatic.

9. __F__ Difficulties do not come to a family in covenant with God.

10. ___T___ God wants His people to be light to the world.

Chapter Six

Answer Sheet

Name:
Class:
Period:
Date:

Read each question carefully, then write (T) for true and (F) for false on the line next to the question.

1. __T__ Order and responsibility in the family must be explained (understood) in order to be effective.

2. __F__ The Biblical perspective of family life is important only for some Christian families.

3. __T__ There are at least four family relationship types in America.

4. __F__ Regardless, of the family type or make-up, children do not need parents to grow healthy; physically, mentally, emotionally, and spiritually.

5. __T__ God has given instruction in the Bible about family roles & responsibilities.

6. __F__ Children receive the same mental and emotional compensations from mother and father.

7. __F__ Step-parents have no responsibilities regarding their step-children.

8. __T__ Parents have at least five responsibilities to fulfill according to God's standards for family life.

9. __T__ Fathers help children to have the sense of knowing that they have the ability to make it in life.

10. __T__ Mothers help children to learn how to develop intimacy/closeness with others.

Chapters Seven & Eight

Answer Sheet

Name: _____
Class:_____
Period:_____
Date: _____

Read each question carefully, then print the letter of the correct answer on the line next to the question.

1. __b__ **Family enhancers are**
    a. Improving communication between spouses only.
    b. Suggested aids to enhance family life.
    c. Not necessary.

2. __a__ **Breaking generational curses**
    a. Allows a family to take back legal ground that Satan has stolen.
    b. Only affects attitudes.
    c. Is accomplished through forgiveness.

3. __c__ **The Greek word for God's love is**
    a. Storge
    b. Phileo
    c. Agape

4. __c__ **A love language**
     a. Is foreign language, like Spanish.
     b. The way two people in love talk to each other.
     c. A primary way in which every individual feels loved.

5. __b__ **The five love languages are**
     a. kissing, holding hands, going on a date, engagement, marriage
     b. Words of affirmation, quality time, receiving gifts, acts of service, physical touch.
     c. Spanish, Greek, Latin, French, Hebrew.

6. __c__ **God's Word if followed**
     a. Can improve family life
     b. Won't necessarily improve family life
     c. Improves family life

7. __a__ **Spending time with family**
     a. Is very important to family intimacy.
     b. Is a good thing to do if you have the time.
     c. Doesn't really matter.

8. __b__ **The Sabbath is**
     a. Something that only the Jews engaged in.
     b. The fourth of the Ten Commandments.
     c. Is a day of sleeping and watching movies.

9. __a__ **Care-fronting is**
     a. an alternative to maintaining relationships by confronting in a caring way.
     b. Allows you to win the argument.
     c. Is only for marriages.

10. _a_ **Family communication is effective when**
      a. Clearly understood by all family members.
      b. The family engages in proper eye contact.
      c. Dirty fighting is at a minimal.

Chapter Nine

Answer Sheet

Name: _____

Class: _____

Period: _____

Date: _____

Read each question carefully, then answer accordingly.

1. Give an explanation of good stewardship.

A good steward willingly follows the rules and regulations of the owner who has entrusted him with his possessions.

2. Who is the steward? Who is the owner?

Christians/disciples of Christ are stewards. God is the owner.

3. Stewardship involves a level of____trust____ and____belief____ in the owner.

4. A disciple follows a __disciplined__ __pattern__ of living according to the rules of the One he follows._

5. Regarding finances, a disciplined pattern can be termed a budget or as a

____Godly____ __Family__ __Financial__ __Plan__ .

6. Name at least 5 items included in the type of budget discussed:

1) Immediate Family 2) Tithe   3) Mother & Father 4) Outreach to poor , fatherless, and widows (including single parents) 5) Taxes 6) Preacher 7) Pleasure 8) Savings & Investing 9) Family Widows

7. The 10% or tithe is optional and depends on whether or not you trust the preacher. (circle the correct answer)

True   (False)

8. Quote one Bible verse or passage mentioned in this chapter:

I Timothy 6:10 , Deuteronomy 12:5-8, 12-13, Matthew 6:33, Matthew 13:11-12, Deuteronomy 8:18, Philippians 4:13, Genesis 14:20, Hebrew 7:2, Malachi 3:10, Exodus 23:19, I Kings 5, Haggai 1, Mark 12:14-17, I Corinthians 9:13-14, I Timothy 5:8, I Timothy 5: 3-4, Matthew 15: 4-6, James 1:27, Galatians 2:10, Isaiah 58:6-7, Ecclesiastes3:13, Luke 14:28, Matthew 25:14-17, Galatians 6:7, James 1:25

9. Wealth includes:

a) money **b)** riches **c)** resources (and land, strength, goods, power, substance)

10. Obeying God's commands brings   blessings   and wealth.

Chapter Ten

Answer Sheet

Name: _____

Class: _____

Period: _____

Date: _____

Read each question carefully, then print the letter of the correct answer on the line next to the question.

1. Name the nine fruit of the Holy Spirit.

   <u>Love, joy, peace, patience (longsuffering), kindness, goodness, faith (faithfulness), meekness (gentleness), temperance (self-control)</u>

2. Give a definition or description of two fruit. <u>See pages 56-60</u>

3. I Corinthians 13:4-8 discusses God's
   <u>Love and its' characteristics</u>

4. The flesh is
   <u>the sinful nature or at odds with the spirit</u>

5. God's desire in the beginning was that man be <u>fruitful and multiply</u>

6. Two Scriptural passages are said to correlate with one another regarding God's love. Name them.

   a)_____Galatians 5:22___ and b)_I Corinthians 13:4-8___

7. Knowing the fruit of the Holy Spirit is important, but _apply-ing them_ is more important.

8. The difference between the Holy Spirit and any other spirit is that it is____Holy_____

9. Why is it of no coincidence that love is the first fruit mentioned?

   Because God is Love, because the Fruit operate through love___

10. When the fruit of the Spirit are in operation, who are we most like?___Jesus___

Chapter Eleven

Answer Sheet

Name: _____
Class:_____
Period:_____
Date: _____

In 2 to 5 paragraphs write specific areas and ways in which your family has or plans to move from ungodly family living to the godly living that God desires for you. Use an additional page, if necessary.

Choose a topic or suggestion from the one of the chapters (Chapters 6, 7, and 11 give suggestions) then elaborate specifically and personally, i.e., how you will apply it to your family life.

Chapter Twelve

Answer Sheet

Name: _____

Class:_____

Period: _____

Date: _____

Use this list as a focus tool. Complete one suggestion at a time. Prioritize according to your family needs. Wait to work on the next suggestion once it has been completed and implemented. Give them time to germinate, root, and grow into fully alive plants in the lives of your family members.

• Develop a family mission statement with goals and put it into action

• As a proactive measure, look at ways to incorporate God's love and the fruit of the Holy Spirit to specific issues that your family is challenged by

• Personally, begin to yield to the biblical role that God has ordained for you

• Teach and model for your children character traits that exemplify godliness

• Read through the Bible with an aim to understand God's love and promises to you and your family

- Spend time in prayer for your family asking God to show you His purpose/call for each family member and write it down - use as a tool of encouragement

- Work on a particular family enhancer to help your family life become more fruitful

- Respond to past ungodly patterns of behavior with repentance (working on completely turning from that behavior) or to hurts or sins against you with forgiveness; name them (see Appendix II)

- If necessary, enlist the aid of a pastoral or Christian counselor to help steer your family in the right direction. Explain what your goals will be.

- Attend a seminar, read a book, listen to teaching tapes or watch videos that can help you and/or your family deal with issues specific to your family members

- Incorporate family prayer and intercession into your family life ("a family that prays together, stays together")

- Adjust your family financial affairs to a God-conscious stewardship plan

APPENDICES

APPENDIX I

TIPS TO HEALTHY/GODLY FAMILY RELATIONSHIPS

- Put God and His ways first, always

- Make sure that the family spends time together

- Deal with unrealistic expectations when conflicts arise

- Observe the attitude and behavior of other family members in different situations to learn their likes and dislikes

- Be honest with yourself and with the family member in conversation

- Communicate - talk about the things that confuse or upset you

- Do not pretend to be what you think they want - be yourself

- Resolve conflict in healthy ways

- Flee from behavior not pleasing to God

- Physical violence is inappropriate family behavior

- Family members putting one another down means that there are unresolved family problems

- Don't be so caught up with how the family looks to outsiders, how influential your family might be, your possessions, or money that you overlook the fact these things do not make a family relationship positive

- Your children count - talk to them, listen to them, include them in discussions when appropriate

- Talk to a mature and godly adult who keeps confidences, about the problems in the relationship to get a healthy viewpoint

- Periodically examine yourself and your relationship with God, with yourself, with your family members

- If there is a lot of tension, arguing and negative attitudes amongst family members, seek spiritual or professional guidance

©2000 Rosalind M. Stanley

APPENDIX II

FORGIVENESS/REPENTANCE

Forgiving:

- Is not condoning the sinful behavior
- Does not mean that you have to be friends with or continue in relationship with the one that sinned against you, though if reconciliation is possible, this should be an ultimate goal.
- Does mean that you do not seek revenge. "Vengeance is Mine, I will repay, says the Lord." (Romans 12:19)
- The person (s) who sinned against you does not mean that you are then left as the responsible person, that you are the blame, or that you are at fault.
- Does not mean that God does not care about you. Forgiving is His plan to help you in receiving His care, covering, and love.
- Does not mean that you are unworthy or deserved it.
- Does mean that you have chosen to obey God, which implies your decision to trust Him.
- Means that you choose (even if reluctantly) to release the person, thus releasing yourself from the negative connection that you have had with them.
- Is not healing.
- Opens the door to healing.
- Is not a feeling, it is an act of obedience to God that operates through His power.
- Does not mean that you did not forgive if continued negative feelings persist after forgiveness. It means that you are in need of healing and deliverance from the effects of the trauma that you experienced. Seeking a Bible-based counselor to assist in this process may be necessary.
- Is a command; unforgiveness counts as sin. (Mark 11:24, 25)

Repentance:

- Is acknowledging your sins against God, others, or yourself.

(Often our response to someone hurting us is an inner sinful response, i.e. attitudes that do not please God.)

- Is humbling yourself before God, thus letting go of pride.
- Enables you entrance into or to regain closeness to God's Kingdom and His Kingdom plans. (see Matthew 3:1,2; Matthew 4:17; Mark 6:7, 12)
- Speaks of a heart yielded to God
- Means dying to self and selfish desires, desires of the flesh, and putting your hope and trust in God and His love and care for you.
- Leads to inner freedom and brings about the joy of the Lord.
- Makes way to receiving healing form God.
- Allows greater closeness and sensitivity to God and His way of doing things.
- Is a command; without it, we choose separation from God.

©2001 Rosalind M. Stanley

APPENDIX III

BIBLICAL FAMILY ROLES
Scriptural Review

HUSBAND

Genesis 2:24

24 Therefore shall a man leave his father and his mother, and shall cleave unto his wife: and they shall be one flesh. (KJV)

Colossians 3:19

19 Husbands, love your wives, and be not bitter against them. (KJV)

Ephesians 5:25-28

25 Husbands, love your wives, even as Christ also loved the church, and gave himself for it;

26 That he might sanctify and cleanse it with the washing of water by the word,

27 That he might present it to himself a glorious church, not having spot, or wrinkle, or any such thing; but that it should be holy and without blemish. 28 So ought men to love their wives as their own bodies. He that loveth his wife loveth himself. (KJV)

1 Peter 3:7

7 Likewise, ye husbands, dwell with them according to knowledge, giving honour unto the wife, as unto the weaker vessel, and as being heirs together of the grace of life; that your prayers be not hindered. (KJV)

I Timothy 3:5

5 (For if a man know not how to rule his own house, how shall he take care of the church of God?) (KJV)

I Timothy 5:8

8 But if any provide not for his own, and specially for those of his own house, he hath denied the faith, and is worse than an infidel. (KJV)

WIFE

Genesis 2:20

20 And Adam gave names to all cattle, and to the fowl of the air, and to every beast of the field; but for Adam there was not found an help meet for him. (KJV)

Ephesians 5:22-24

22 Wives, submit yourselves unto your own husbands, as unto the Lord.

23 For the husband is the head of the wife, even as Christ is the head of the church: and he is the Saviour of the body.

24 Therefore as the church is subject unto Christ, so let the wives be to their own husbands in every thing. (KJV)

Proverbs 31:11-12

11 The heart of her husband doth safely trust in her, so that he shall have no need of spoil.

12 She will do him good and not evil all the days of her life. (KJV)

1 Peter 3:1-6

1 Likewise, ye wives, be in subjection to your own husbands; that, if any obey not the word, they also may without the word be won by the conversation of the wives;

2 While they behold your chaste conversation coupled with fear.

3 Whose adorning let it not be that outward adorning of plaiting the hair, and of wearing of gold, or of putting on of apparel;

4 But let it be the hidden man of the heart, in that which is not

corruptible, even the ornament of a meek and quiet spirit, which is in the sight of God of great price.

5 For after this manner in the old time the holy women also, who trusted in God, adorned themselves, being in subjection unto their own husbands:

6 Even as Sara obeyed Abraham, calling him lord: whose daughters ye are, as long as ye do well, and are not afraid with any amazement. (KJV)

FATHER

Deuteronomy 6:6-7

6 And these words, which I command thee this day, shall be in thine heart:

7 And thou shalt teach them diligently unto thy children, and shalt talk of them when thou sittest in thine house, and when thou walkest by the way, and when thou liest down, and when thou risest up. (KJV)

Deuteronomy 11:19

19 And ye shall teach them your children, speaking of them when thou sittest in thine house, and when thou walkest by the way, when thou liest down, and when thou risest up. (KJV)

Ephesians 6:4

4 And, ye fathers, provoke not your children to wrath: but bring them up in the nurture and admonition of the Lord. (KJV)

Malachi 4:6

And he shall turn the heart of the fathers to the children, and the heart of the children to their fathers, lest I come and smite the earth with a curse. (KJV)

• Father's Living out their God given roles brings the family into godly order-this then leads to a church in godly order

1 Timothy 5:8

8 But if any provide not for his own, and specially for those of his own house, he hath denied the faith, and is worse than an infidel. (KJV)

Proverbs 6:20

20 My son, keep thy father's commandment, and forsake not the law of thy mother: (KJV)

Colossians 3:21

21 Fathers, provoke not your children to anger, lest they be discouraged. (KJV)

Proverbs 22:6

6 Train up a child in the way he should go: and when he is old, he will not depart from it. (KJV)

Proverbs 22:18

18 For it is a pleasant thing if thou keep them within thee; they shall withal be fitted in thy lips. (KJV)

MOTHER

Deuteronomy 6:6-7

6 And these words, which I command thee this day, shall be in thine heart:

7 And thou shalt teach them diligently unto thy children, and shalt talk of them when thou sittest in thine house, and when thou walkest by the, and when thou liest down, and when thou risest up. (KJV)

Proverbs 6:20

20 My son, keep thy father's commandment, and forsake not the law of thy mother: (KJV)

Proverbs 22:6

    6 Train up a child in the way he should go: and when he is old, he will not depart from it. (KJV)

Proverbs 22:18

    18 For it is a pleasant thing if thou keep them within thee; they shall withal be fitted in thy lips. (KJV)

Proverbs 31:27-28

    27 She looketh well to the ways of her household, and eateth not the bread of idleness.

    28 Her children arise up, and call her blessed; her husband also, and he praiseth her. (KJV)

PARENTS (& STEPPARENTS)

Deuteronomy 6:6-7

    6 And these words, which I command thee this day, shall be in thine heart:

    7 And thou shalt teach them diligently unto thy children, and shalt talk of them when thou sittest in thine house, and when thou walkest by the way, and when thou liest down, and when thou risest up. (KJV)

Deuteronomy 11:19

    19 And ye shall teach them your children, speaking of them when thou sittest in thine house, and when thou walkest by the way, when thou liest down, and when thou risest up. (KJV)

Proverbs 22:6

    6 Train up a child in the way he should go: and when he is old, he will not depart from it. (KJV)

Proverbs 22:18

18 For it is a pleasant thing if thou keep them within thee; they shall withal be fitted in thy lips. (KJV)

CHILDREN

Exodus 20:12

12 Honour thy father and thy mother: that thy days may be long upon the land which the LORD thy God giveth thee. (KJV)

Deuteronomy 5:16

16 Honour thy father and thy mother, as the LORD thy God hath commanded thee; that thy days may be prolonged, and that it may go well with thee, in the land which the LORD thy God giveth thee. (KJV)

Proverbs 1:8

8 My son, hear the instruction of thy father, and forsake not the law of thy mother: (KJV)

Proverbs 6:20

20 My son, keep thy father's commandment, and forsake not the law of thy mother: (KJV)

FAMILY

1 Peter 3:8

8 Finally, be ye all of one mind, having compassion one of another, love as brethren, be pitiful, be courteous: (KJV)

Ephesians 5:21

21 Submitting yourselves one to another in the fear of God. (KJV)

Deuteronomy 29:18-22

18 Lest there should be among you man, or woman, or family, or tribe, whose heart turneth away this day from the LORD our God, to go and serve the gods of these nations; lest there should be among you a root that beareth gall and wormwood;... (KJV)

Genesis 17:14

14 And the uncircumcised man child whose flesh of his foreskin is not circumcised, that soul shall be cut off from his people; he hath broken my covenant. (KJV)

Proverbs 29:18

18 Where there is no vision, the people perish: but he that keepeth the law, happy is he. (KJV)

Isaiah 26:20

20 Come, my people, enter thou into thy chambers, and shut thy doors about thee: hide thyself as it were for a little moment, until the indignation be overpast. (KJV)

Mark 7:6

6 He answered and said unto them, Well hath Esaias prophesied of you hypocrites, as it is written, This people honoureth me with their lips, but their heart is far from me. (KJV)

Luke 1:17

17 And he shall go before him in the spirit and power of Elias, to turn the hearts of the fathers to the children, and the disobedient to the wisdom of the just; to make ready a people prepared for the Lord. (KJV)

1 Peter 2:9

9 But ye are a chosen generation, a royal priesthood, an holy nation, a peculiar people; that ye should shew forth the praises of him who hath called you out of darkness into his marvellous light: (KJV)

Revelations 21:3

3 And I heard a great voice out of heaven saying, Behold, the tabernacle of God is with men, and he will dwell with them, and they shall be his people, and God himself shall be with them, and be their God. (KJV)

Ephesians 6:1-3

1 Children, obey your parents in the Lord: for this is right.
2 Honour thy father and mother; (which is the first command-ment with promise;)
3 That it may be well with thee, and thou mayest live long on the earth. (KJV)

Colossians 3:20

20 Children, obey your parents in all things: for this is well pleasing unto the Lord. (KJV)

APPENDIX IV

Parenting Tips

- *Take care of yourself:*
  exercise, healthy eating, social activity, spiritual training

- *Don't expect to know everything about parenting*

- *Be willing to ask for help*

- *Entrust your children to God*

- *Allow for family (parent/child) fun time*

- *Realize that your best is good enough*

- *Develop a family routine:*
  set bedtimes, mealtimes, wake-up time, etc.

- *Remember that all parents make mistakes:*
  forgive yourself quickly

- *Make sure that your children know that you are the parent and not their friend*

- *Read books and magazines about child development*

- *Pray for wisdom & creativity*

- *Refrain from yelling or screaming to get your child to obey*

- *Develop a discipline procedure; this will help lessen anger responses*

- *Remind yourself daily that your child is the priority*

- *Make your lifestyle as simple as possible*

- *Try hard not to live above your income*

- *When stressed or overwhelmed, use stress reduction techniques: deep breathing, time-out, tensing & relaxing muscles, prayer, music*

- *Develop friendships with other loving and caring parents*

"Point your kids in the right direction-when they're old they won't be lost"

©1996 Rosalind M. Caldwell

APPENDIX V

The Be Awares...

* *being too serious - laughter is good medicine*

* *taking your frustrations out on your child(ren)*

* *attempts to overcompensate*

* *trying to be both mom and dad*

* *living your life through your child*

* *being too busy to "be there" emotionally and mentally for your child (ren)*

* *using the television or video games as baby-sitter*

* *differences in your children's personalities and emotional needs*

* *being too strict or too lenient*

* *other adults (or children) that may negatively affect your child(ren)*

* *the fact that structure is healthy*

* *hugs: both you and your child need them*

* *lecturing without listening*

* *not enjoying your child (ren)*

* *taking time to let your child (ren) know that you care*

* *expecting your child (ren) to act like an adult*

* *setting the right example in front of your child (ren)*

* *teaching and training your child (ren): education begins at home*

* *appropriate discipline is an act of love/lack shows that you don't care*

IT DOESN'T TAKE MUCH TO BECOME A PARENT - BEING A PARENT IS WHAT COUNTS

©1996 Rosalind M. Caldwell

APPENDIX VI

DIRTY FIGHTING TACTICS

From: PAIRS International, <u>www.pairs.org.</u>

- Bringing up more than one issue or complaint at a time

- Bullying

- Contempt

- Criticizing

- Lying

- Humiliating

- Labeling

- Mimicking, Mocking

- Mind-reading or "psychoanalyzing" your partner or loved one

- Name-calling

- Ordering

- Sarcasm

- Switching the subject with counter accusations (blaming) or diversions (distracting)

- Taunting, Ridiculing

- Threatening

- Using "cold logic" to hide from emotional reality

- Complaining

- Denying

- Disqualifying

- Forgetting

- Breaking Promises

- Playing Confused

- Dragging Your Feet

- Exaggeration (You always...)

- Keeping Score

- Making Excuses

- Playing Poor Me

- Playing The Martyr

- Playing the Victim

- Pretending Your Partner is Being Unreasonable

- Stonewalling (I'm not talking to you)

- Withholding

- Yelling or Screaming

- Others_____

APPENDIX VII

GODLY   vs.   UNGODLY

Christlike Virtue (Galatians 5:22)	Opposite	Perversion
Love	Hate/lust*	Permissiveness/ selfishness or self-centeredness
Joy	Pain/grief*	Preoccupation with gratification, frenzy
Peace	War	Neutrality
Longsuffering	Impatience	Lenience
Gentleness	Hardness	Softness
Goodness	Badness	Finicky, nice
Faithfulness	Faithlessness	Legalism
Meekness	Arrogance	Weakness
Temperance/ Self-control	Undisciplined/ self-indulgent	Fleshy effort or self-effort

From: Hunt, T.W., **The Mind of Christ**, Broadman & Holman Publishers, 1995.
* extra word added by this author

References

Augsburger, David, <u>Caring Enough to Confront:</u> How to Understand and Express Our Deepest Feelings Toward Others, Herald Press, 1973.

<u>www.aahmi.org</u> African American Healthy Marriage Initiative, Administration for Children & Families, Washington, DC, 2004

<u>American Heritage Dictionary:</u> Second College Edition, Houghton Mifflin, 1982.

Banks, W. L., <u>The Black Church in the U.S.: It's Origin, Growth, Contribution, and Outlook</u>, Moody press, Chicago, IL, 1972.

Bennett, Lerone, <u>The Shaping of Black America</u>, Penquin Books, New York, NY, 1993.

Billingsley, A, <u>Climbing Jacob's Ladder</u>, Simon Schuster Touchstone Books, 1990.

Boone, Wellington, *"Revival in the Inner City—God's Answer to Genocide in the Black Community,"* Richmond, VA, 1990.

<u>www.blackwomenshealth.org</u> Black Women's Health Imperative, *NBWHP Fact Sheet: African American Women and Adolescent Pregnancy*, Washington, D.C., 2001.

Booker, Richard, <u>The Miracle of The Scarlet Thread</u>, Logos International, 1981.

Chapman, Gary, <u>The Five Love Languages</u>, Northfield Publishing, Chicago, IL, 1992.

Christenson, Larry, <u>The Christian Family</u>, Bethany House Publishers, Minneapolis, MN, 1970.

Cloud, Henry and Townsend, John, <u>The Mom Factor</u>, Zondervan Publishing, Grand Rapids, MI, 1996.

Cole, Edwin Louis, <u>Maximized Manhood: A Guide To Family Survival</u>, Whitaker House, 2000.

Collins, Gary R., <u>How to be a People Helper,</u> Tyndale House Publishers, 1995.

Dewart, J., ED., <u>The State of Black America</u>, National Urban League, New York, NY, 1990.

Evans, Anthony, <u>Guiding Your Family in a Misguided World</u>, Focus on the Family Publishing, Pomana, CA, 1991.

Franklin, J. H., <u>From Slavery to Freedom: A History of Negro Americans</u>, Alfred A. Knopf, Inc., 1980.

Frazier, E. F., <u>The Negro Church in America</u>, Schocken Books, New York, NY, 1963.

Frazier, E. F., <u>The Negro Family in the United States</u>, The University of Chicago, IL, 1966.

Gordon, Lori, <u>PEERS: Skills for Emotional Intimacy</u>, PAIRS Foundation, Ltd., 1999.

Hunt, T.W., <u>The Mind of Christ</u>, Broadman & Holman Publishers, 1995.

Jakes, Thomas Dexter, *Admit It, Quit It, Forget It*, TD Jakes Ministries, Audio/Video, 1997

Jeremiah, David, <u>God in You: Releasing the Power of the Holy Spirit in Your Life</u>, Multnomah Publishers, 1998.

Kylstra, Chester and Betsy, <u>Restoring the Foundations: Counseling by the Living Word</u>, Proclaiming His Word, Inc., PO Box 2339, Santa Rosa Beach, FL, 1996.

Lincoln, C. E., and Mamiya, L. H., The Black Church in African American Experience, Duke University Press, Durham and London, 1990.

MacArthur, John Jr., Your Family, Moody Press, Chicago, IL, 1982.

Matthew Henry Commentary on the Whole Bible: New Modern Edition, electronic database, Hendrickson Publishers, 1991. (PC Bible Study)

McGee, Robert, Father Hunger, Servant Publication, Ann Arbor, MI, 1993.

Merriam-Webster Collegiate Dictionary: Tenth Edition, 1994.

Murray, Andrew, Abide in Christ, BPCC Hazell Books, 1990.

Newton, H. M., Can The Black family Be Saved?, African American Evangelical Press, Monterey, CA, 1988.

Orr, Jean, Biblical Counseling, Holman Bible Publishers, Nashville, TN, 1989.

Prince, Derek, God is a Matchmaker, Chosen Books, Old Tappan, NJ, 1984.

Prince, Derek, The Marriage Covenant, Whitaker House, 1978.

Rekers, George, A., Counseling Families, Word Publishing, Dallas, TX, 1988.

Sandford, John and Paula, Restoring the Christian Family, Victory House, Inc., Tulsa, OK. 1979.

Schlink, M. Basilea, Repentance - The Joy-Filled Life, Bethany House Publishers, 1984.

Strong's Exhaustive Concordance of the Bible, Dugan Publishers, 1894.

The Comparative Study Bible: A Parallel Bible, Zondervan Publishing House, 1984.

Verwer, George, The Revolution of Love, STL Books, 1989.

Vine, W. E., Vine's Expository Dictionary of Old and New Testament

Words, Fleming H. Revell Company, 1981.

Walker, Clarence, <u>Biblical Counseling With African Americans</u>, Zondervan Publishing, Grand Rapids, MI, 1992.

Winter, R.D. and Hawthorne, S. C., Eds, <u>Perspectives on the World Christian Movement</u>, Carey Library, Pasadena, CA, 1981.

Wright, H. Norman, <u>Communication: The Key to Your Marriage,</u> Regal Books. 1974

Suggested Reading

Book Title	Author
Abide in Christ	Andrew Murray
Blended Families	Maxine Marsolini
Can Step Families Be Done Right?	Joann & Seth Webster
Can Two Walk Together And Agree	Sabrina Black
Caring Enough To Confront	David Augsburger
Father Hunger	Robert S. McGee
Financial Peace Planner (for family Financial Health)	Dave Ramsey
Growing Kids God's Way	Gary & Anne Ezzo
Help, I'm Raising My Children Alone	T.D. Jakes
How to Love a Black Man/Woman (these are 2 separate books)	Ronn Elmore
Transforming Your Relationships	Ronn Elmore
Marital Secrets: Dating, Communication and Sex	Paris Finner-Williams
Maximized Manhood	Edwin Louis Cole
Parenting the Hurt Child (for Adoptive Families)	Keck, Kupecky, Mansfiled
Parenting With Loving Limits	Bruce Narramore
Practicing the Presence of God	Brother Lawrence

Raising Emotionally Healthy Kids	Wright & Oliver
Restoring the Black Family	Willie Richardson
Restoring The Christian Family	John & Paula Sandford
Sacred Marriage	Gary Thomas
The Art of Friendship	Ted W. Engstrom
The Battle for the Seed	Patricia Morgan
The Blessing	Smalley & Trent
The Christian Family	Larry Christenson
The Complete Marriage & Family Home Reference Guide	James C. Dobson
The Family Manager's Guide for Working Moms	Kathy Peel
The Great Investment	T.D. Jakes
The Marriage Covenant	Derek Prince
The Miracle of the Scarlet Thread	Richard Booker
The Mystery of Marriage	Mike Mason
The Power of a Praying Parent (Wife/Husband) (these are 3 separate books)	Stormie Omartian
The Purpose of a Woman (Man) (these are 2 separate books)	Myles Munroe
The Smart Stepfamily	Ron Deal
The Successful Family	Creflo & Taffy Dollar
Trusting: Learning Who & How to Trust Again	Pat Springle
Woman, Wife, Mother	Patricia Harrison
Your Money Counts	Howard Dayton
Your Wife Can Be your Best Friend	Clarence Shuler

Author Information

Rosalind M. (Caldwell) Stanley received her Masters of Arts degree in Counseling from Regent University (formerly CBN University), Virginia Beach, Virginia; one of the premier Christian graduate schools in the nation. She has over 15 years experience combined as a lay and professional counselor and several years of effective leadership in various senior level positions. Her personal life experiences of abuse in her childhood, gang involvement and pregnancy at 13, as well as other life challenges, add to her ability to effectively assist hurting people. She is a gifted workshop presenter, diligent and excellent in ministry and program development and an anointed Biblically based motivational speaker to youth and adults. Roz serves as First Vice Chairperson for BAACC (Black African American Christian Counselors), a division of the American Association of Christian Counselors (AACC), member and former board member of the DFW Healthy Marriage & Family Coalition, member of the Dallas Area Initiative for Healthy African American Marriages & Families, board member of the National Alliance for the Mentally Ill-Dallas Affiliate, Member of the City of Lancaster, TX- Human Relations Commission, and member of the Dallas Faith-based Abstinence Alliance. Her ministry focus and purpose is helping hurting people in receiving healing and making changes necessary for a productive life. Roz provides consulting and training for those called to help the hurting, covering a variety

of topics. She also conducts seminars, workshops and groups for the hurting individual or family. Roz is currently in the process of establishing a home for troubled girls; BECAUSE OF GRACE HOPE CENTER, a 501(c) (3), nonprofit, nonpartisan, interdenominational, residential & nonresidential ministry. She is mother to Victoria and Jason, step- mother to Arthur Lee and Nathan, mother-in-law to Ruben and has been blessed with seven precious grandchildren. She and her husband, Arthur, reside in the Dallas area of Texas.

OTHER BOOKS TO BE RELEASED
BY THIS AUTHOR:

BEWISER in the Workplace: Work Ethics for Christians

STRESS INDICATION TEST: An Informal Tool to Help Christians Reduce Stress

BECAUSE of GRACE: My Journey to Wholeness After Abuse & Pregnancy at 13

FAMILY LIFE: Dealing With The Hard Stuff (Issue Focused)

LIFE VS. DEATH CYCLE: Let Us Not Be Deceived

We trust that this book has been beneficial to you. If you would like additional copies or further information about our consulting & training services, or to schedule a workshop or speaking engagement please contact us at:

Because Of Grace™

Consulting & Training Services
PO Box 356
Lancaster, TX 75134
Or
Email us at:
RozBOG@aol.com

If you are interested in learning more about
BECAUSE OF GRACE HOPE CENTER
Ministry & Services
for
Girls in Troubling Situations
Visit us on the Web:
www.becauseofgracehopecenter.org